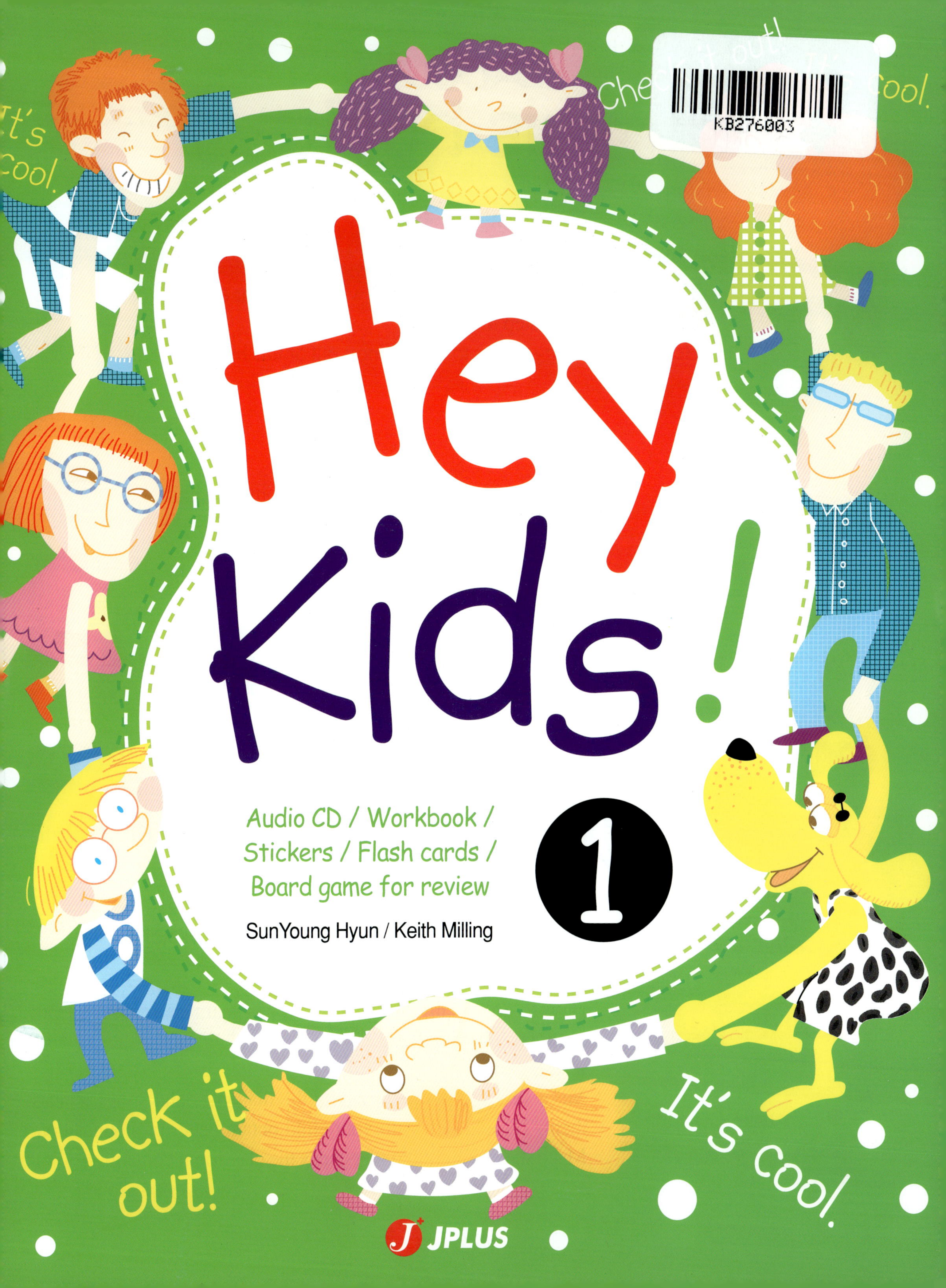

Hey Kids!
Audio CD / Workbook / Stickers / Flash cards / Board game for review
SunYoung Hyun / Keith Milling
1
Check it out!
It's cool!
JPLUS
KB276003

About this book

Thank you for purchasing *Hey Kids!* It will allow your child to take his or her first step in English.
Here are some suggestions to get the most out of this book.

Dialogue — There are up to four key sentences from each unit.

Listen and repeat — One more step! Repeat and practice the sentences.

Phonics — You can learn how to pronounce English consonants and vowels. You can also practice with a native speaker.

Let's play — You can play interesting games using the sentences you learned. Then, you can practice them in a natural way.

Let's practice — Answer the questions. Check your weak points and review the text.

Let's sing — Sing in English using the key vocabulary and expressions.

Let's learn more — How to do say it in English? You can learn more words from everyday life with drawings.

Audio CD — Make sure your child listens to the dialogues and songs repeats them. The CD will help your child obtain better pronounciation. Make sure your child understands the classroom content.

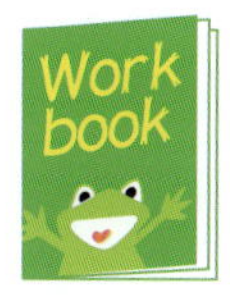

Workbook

Keeping up to date in the activity book and on homework will help your child improve more quickly and get the most out of classes.

Flash cards

You can practice the words from each unit easily and naturally.

Always remember, English is just another way to communicate. It's OK to make it fun and interesting. Instead of forcing children to study hard, let them enjoy English by playing games, reading books, and watching movies. It is very important to get off on the right foot in English when children begin to learn.

Author *Sun Young Hyun*

I am really pleased that I could have the opportunity to write this series. *Hey Kids!* will provide students with the advantages of a well-known, well produced, existing book with updated, contemporary English.

I tried to focus on interests for children including characters, pictures, games and songs. These will allow students to learn naturally.

I know the children will improve a great deal with *Hey Kids!*. I'd like to thank everyone who has helped produce *Hey Kids!*.

Supervisor *Keith Milling*

Welcome to the *Hey Kids!* series. *Hey Kids!* is an introductory, communication based English book for early elementary school students. *Hey Kids!* has everything a child needs to begin their first step in English – likeable characters, games, and activities. And of course *Hey Kids!* contains all of the essential parts a basic for language book for children should: listening, speaking, reading, and writing. *Hey Kids!* will help get your child off to a great start!

Contents

Syllabus

2

1 What do you want?

Key Expression

· What do you want?
  I want some french fries.
· What would you like?
  I'd like a hamburger.

Phonics M
Game What do you want?
Song What do you want?

2 Do you want some more?

Key Expression

· Do you want a fork?
  Yes, please.
· Would you like some more?
  No, thanks.

Phonics N
Game Set the table
Words In the kitchen

3 Where is my bag?

Key Expression

· Where is my cap?
  It's on the chair.

Phonics L
Game Where is the ball?
Song Where is the pencil?

4 Can you swim?

Key Expression

· Can you play soccer?
  Yes, I can.
· Can you ski?
  No, I can't. I cannot ski.

Phonics R
Game Picture puzzle
Song Can you play soccer?

5 How many bees?

Key Expression

· How many stars?
  Twelve stars.

Phonics J
Game Word find
Song Number song

6 He is tall.

Key Expression

· I am short.
  He is tall.
· He is strong.
  I am weak.

Phonics H
Game He is tall.
Song Big and small

7 What do you have?

Key Expression

· What do you have?
  I have two balls.

7 (cont.)

Phonics W
Game What's different?
Song What do you have?

8 Do you have a dog?

Key Expression

· Do you have a turtle?
  Yes, I do. I have two turtles.
· Do you have a rabbit?
  No, I don't.

Phonics Y
Game What is it?
Song Do you have a dog?

9 How's the weather today?

Key Expression

· How's the weather today?
  It's sunny.

Phonics Q
Game Board game
Song Rain rain go away

10 What day is it today?

Key Expression

· What day is it today?
  It's Wednesday.

Phonics X
Game What day is it today?
Song What day is it today?

1 There is one tiger.

Key Expression

· Are there four lions?
No, there aren't. There are two lions.
· How many ostriches?
Three ostriches.

Phonics   Short Vowel A
Game   Make your own zoo
Words   In the sea

2 What does he do?

Key Expression

· What does your mother do?
She's a doctor.

Phonics   Long Vowel A
Game   Crossword puzzle
Words   Jobs

3 Where are you from?

Key Expression

· Where are you from?
I'm from Korea.
· Are you Japanese?
No, I'm not. I'm American.

Phonics   Short Vowel E
Game   Where are you from?
Song   Where are you from?

4 What time is it?

Key Expression

· What time is it?
It's two o'clock.
· What time is it?
It's five thirty.

Phonics   Long Vowel E
Game   What time is it?
Words   In the classroom

5 What are you doing?

Key Expression

· What are you doing?
I'm listening to music.
· What is he doing?
He is sleeping.

Phonics   Short Vowel I
Game   Bingo
Song   What are you doing?

6 How much is it?

Key Expression

· How much is it?
It's two hundred won.

Phonics   Long Vowel I
Game   Role play
Song   How much is it?

7 Where do you live?

Key Expression

· Where do you live?
I live in Manhattan.

· What's your phone number?
It's 432-8516.

Phonics   Short Vowel O
Game   Board game
Song   Where do you live?

8 How do you feel today?

Key Expression

· How do you feel today?
I'm happy.

Phonics   Long Vowel O
Game   Crossword puzzle
Song   How do you feel today?

9 Where are you going?

Key Expression

· Where are you going?
I'm going to the library.

Phonics   Short Vowel U
Game   Find the way
Song   Where are you going?

10 What date is it today?

Key Expression

· What date is it today?
It's December 25th.
It's Christmas!

Phonics   Long Vowel U
Game   Board game
Song   What date is it today?

In the classroom

- What does _______ mean?

- How do you say _______ in English?

- I don't understand.

- I don't know.

- Please help me!

Hannah
Seven
America
May 9th
Female
Taurus
Listening to music

Name
Age
Country
Birthday
Gender
Zodiac
Hobby

Olivia
Seven
Korea
September 2nd
Female
Virgo
Playing the piano

Joshua
eight
Korea
July 10th
Male
Leo
Playing soccer

Ethan
six
China
March 1st
Male
Pisces
Reading

Dusty
three
England
April 8th
Male
Aries
Singing

Hello!

Goodbye!

Bye!

Listen and repeat

④ How are you?
⑤ I'm fine.
⑥ I'm good.
⑩ Goodbye!
⑪ Bye!
Ethan
Olivia
Dusty
1

 **P p** 

pencil

puppy

pan

pig

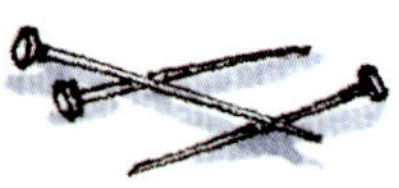

pins

pot

Let's play

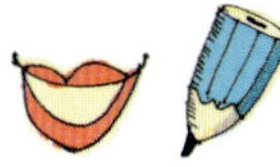

Hello!

Hello!

___________.

Find the correct name. Then, say "Hello, _______."

 ## Let's practice 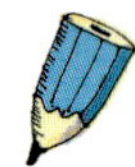

A Listen and number. 04

B Look at the pictures. Write the correct sentences.

① 

②

Bye.
Hello, Hannah!
I'm good.

C Listen and number. 05

   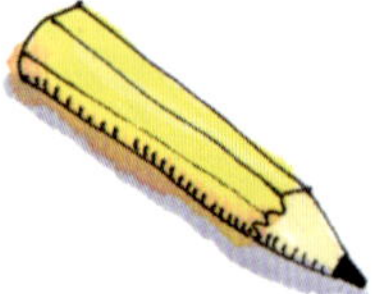

Hello

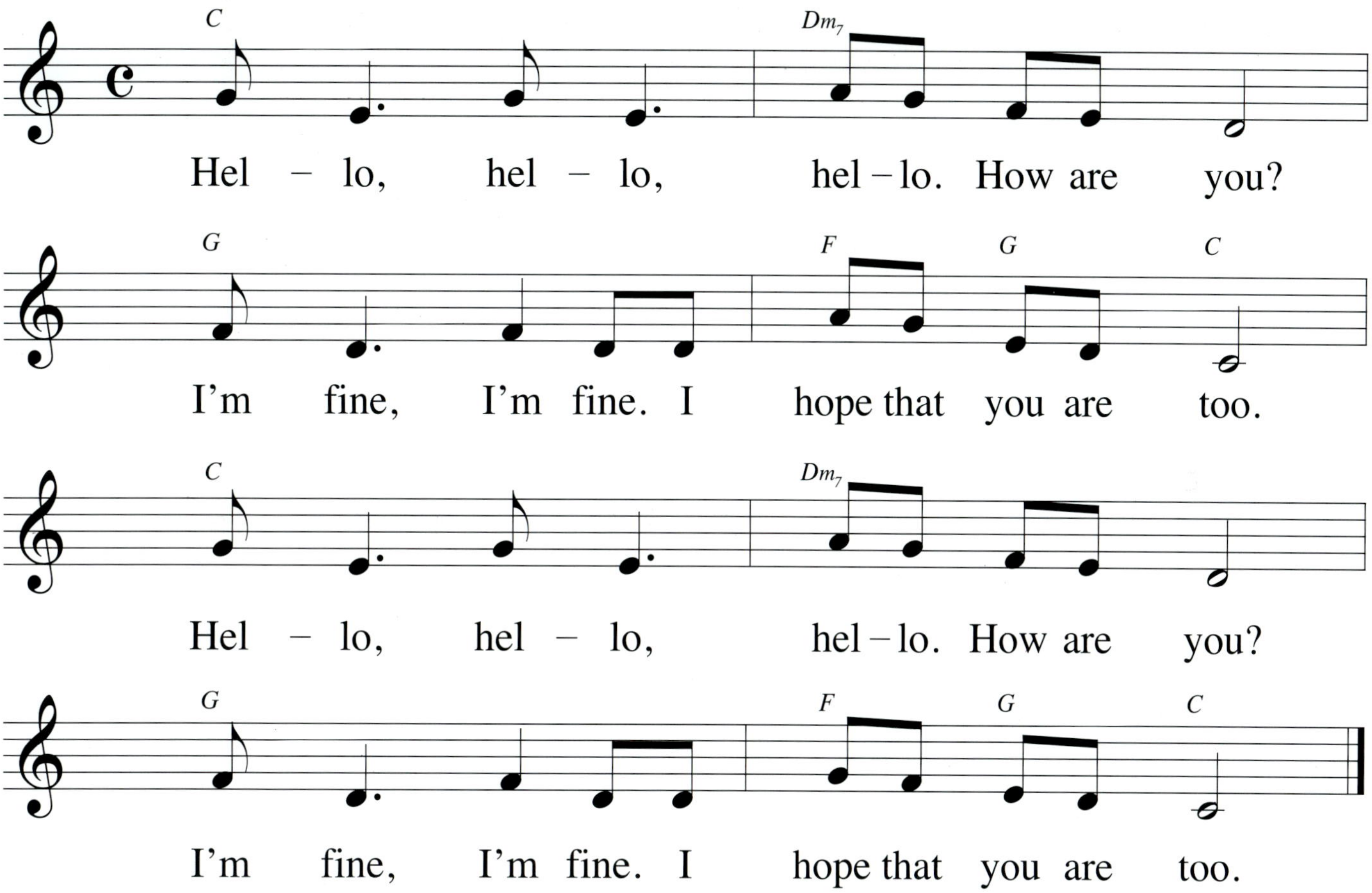

Hel – lo, hel – lo, hel – lo. How are you?

I'm fine, I'm fine. I hope that you are too.

Hel – lo, hel – lo, hel – lo. How are you?

I'm fine, I'm fine. I hope that you are too.

UNIT 2 — Thank you!

Thank you!

You're welcome!

I'm sorry.

That's all right.

① Thank you!
② You're welcome!
③ I'm sorry!
④ That's all right!
⑤ Thanks!
⑥ You're welcome!

⑦ I'm sorry!
⑧ That's all right!
⑨ Thanks!
⑩ You're welcome!
⑪ I'm sorry!
⑫ That's okay!

book

ball

bed

bus

bag

bike

 Let's play

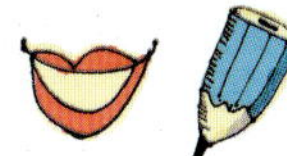

Matching

Happy Birthday!

Help!

Thank you!

I'm sorry!

Draw lines from the pictures to the correct sentences.

Let's practice

A Listen and number.  10

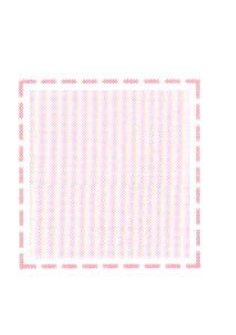

B Look at the pictures. Write the correct sentences.

① 

② 

C Listen and number.  11

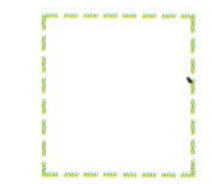

 Let's sing

Thank you

UNIT 3 What is your name?

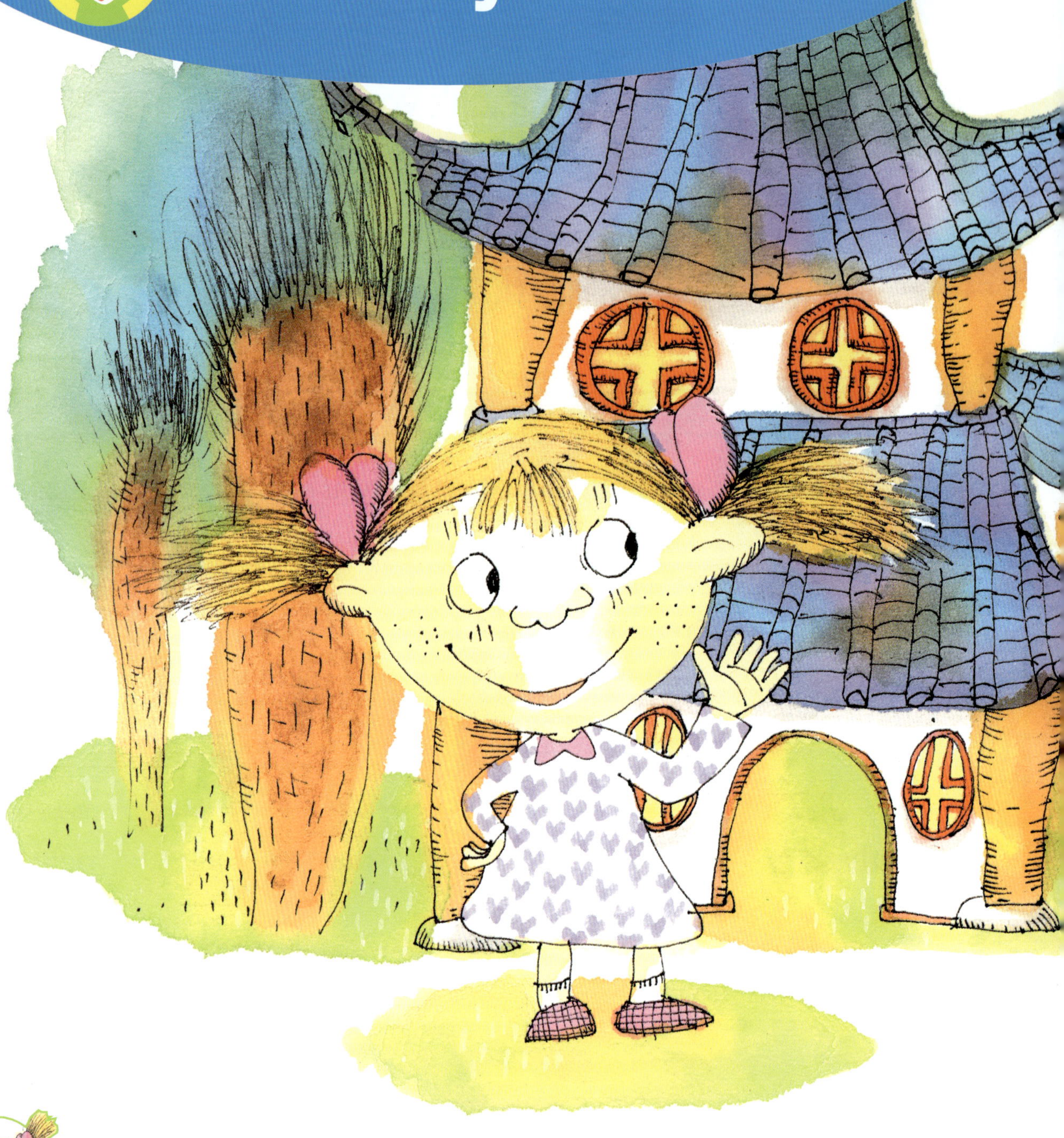

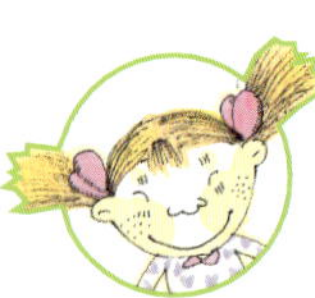

 What is your name?

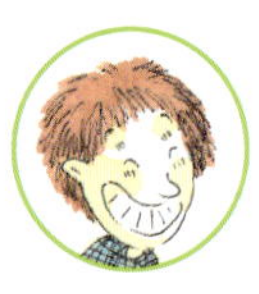

 My name is Joshua. What's your name?

I'm Hannah.

Hi, Hannah!

① What is your name?
④ Hi! My name is Hannah.
⑤ My name is Joshua.
⑥ I'm Dusty.

② I'm Olivia.
③ Hi, Olivia!
⑧ My name is Jacob.
⑦ Hi! I'm Ethan.

T t

tiger

toy

ten

top

tape

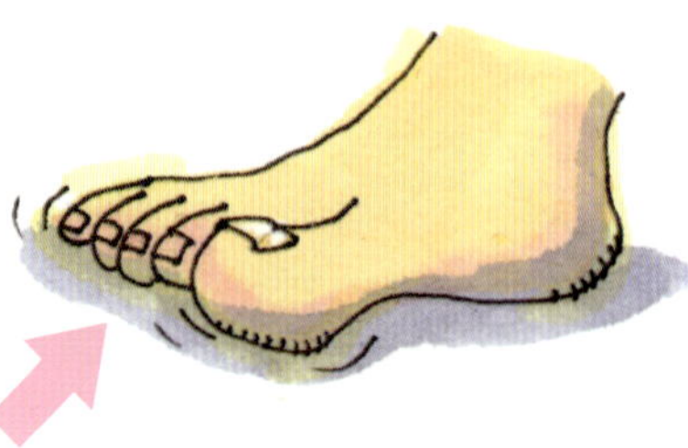

toe

Bingo! Bingo!

Hannah	Joshua	Ethan
Joshua	Hannah	Olivia
Ethan	Joshua	Olivia

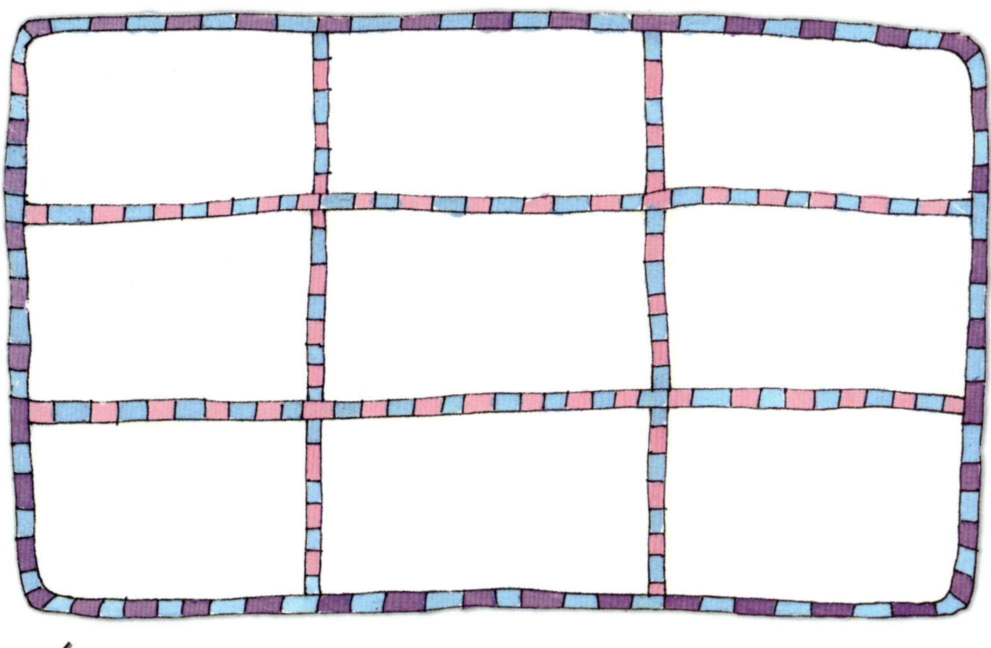

Write character's names in the blanks. Then, play Bingo.

Making a name tag!

Make a name tag.
Draw your face on the name tag and write your name.

Let's practice

A Listen and number.  16

B Work with a partner. Ask and answer.

C Listen and number.  17

Let's sing

What's your name?

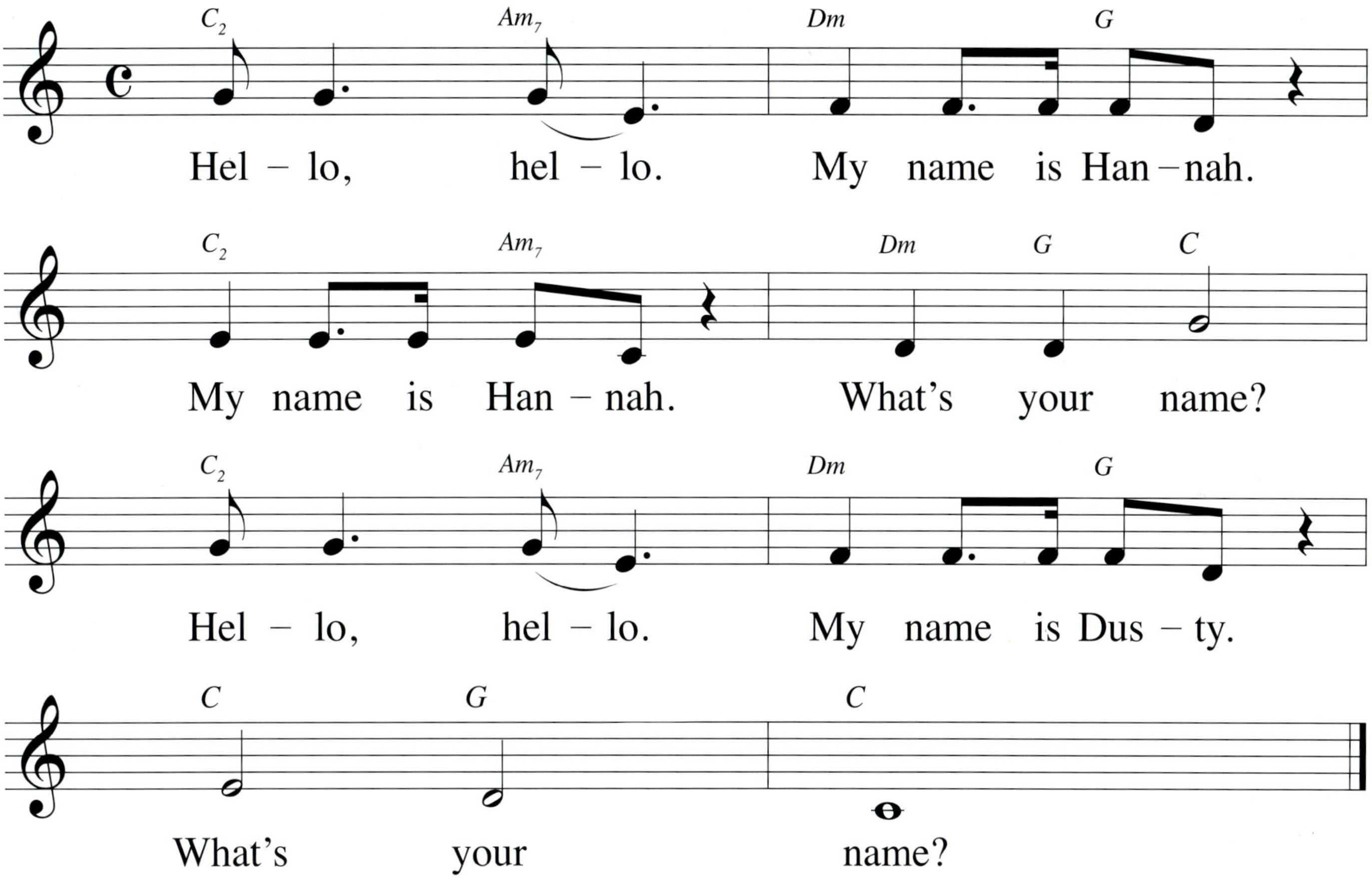

UNIT 4

What is this?

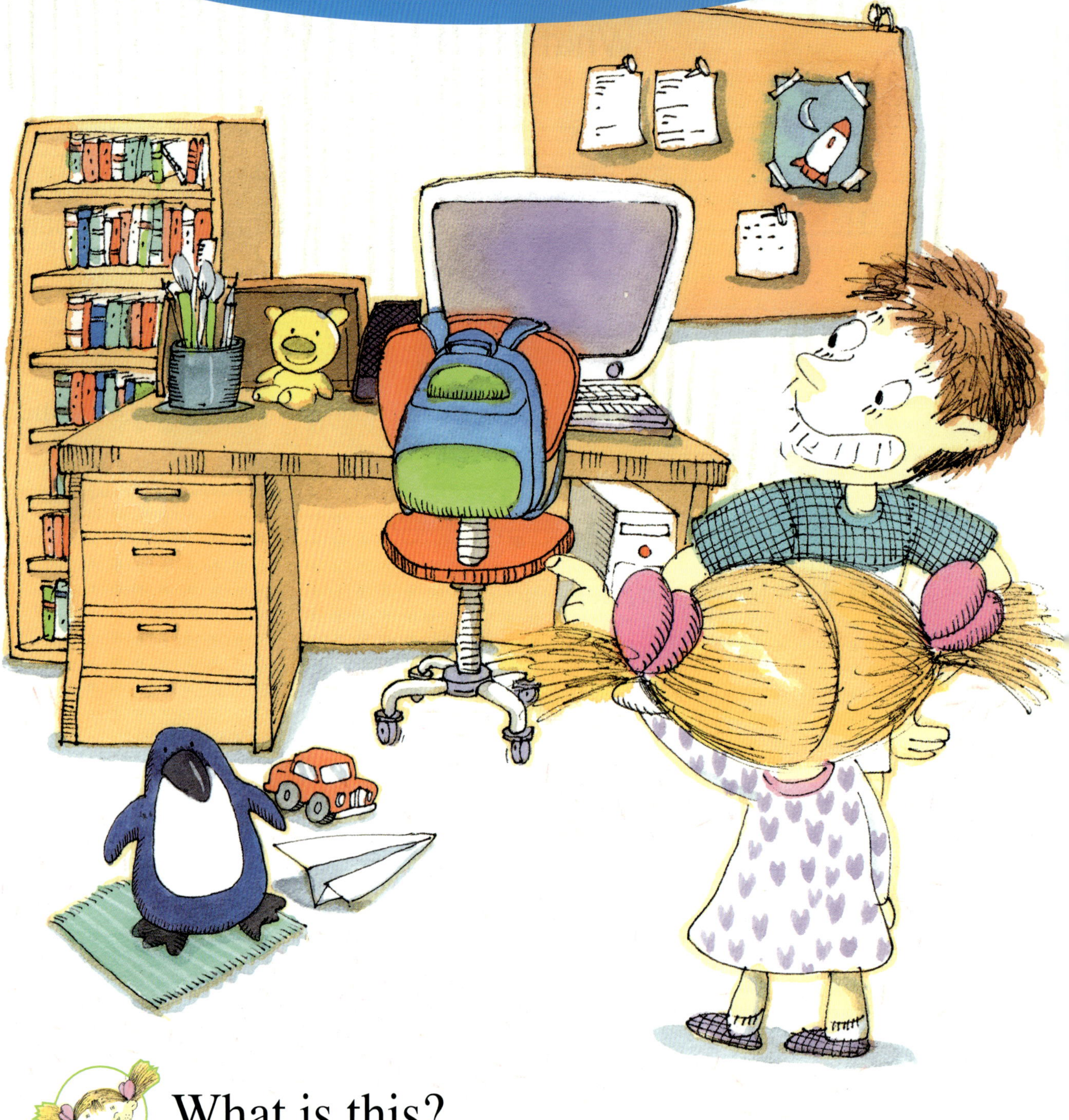

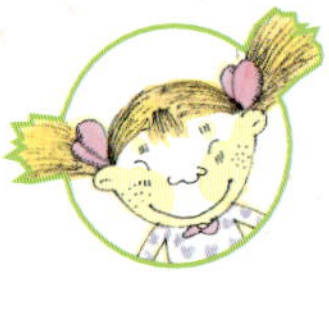

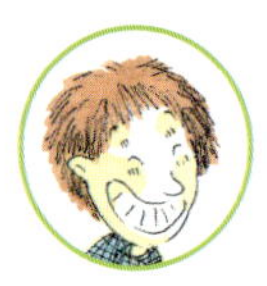

What is this?

This is a bag.

4

What is that?

That is a cap.

① What is this?
② This is a pencil.
③ What are these?
④ These are pencils.
⑤ What is that?
⑥ That is a notebook.
⑦ What are those?
⑧ Those are notebooks.

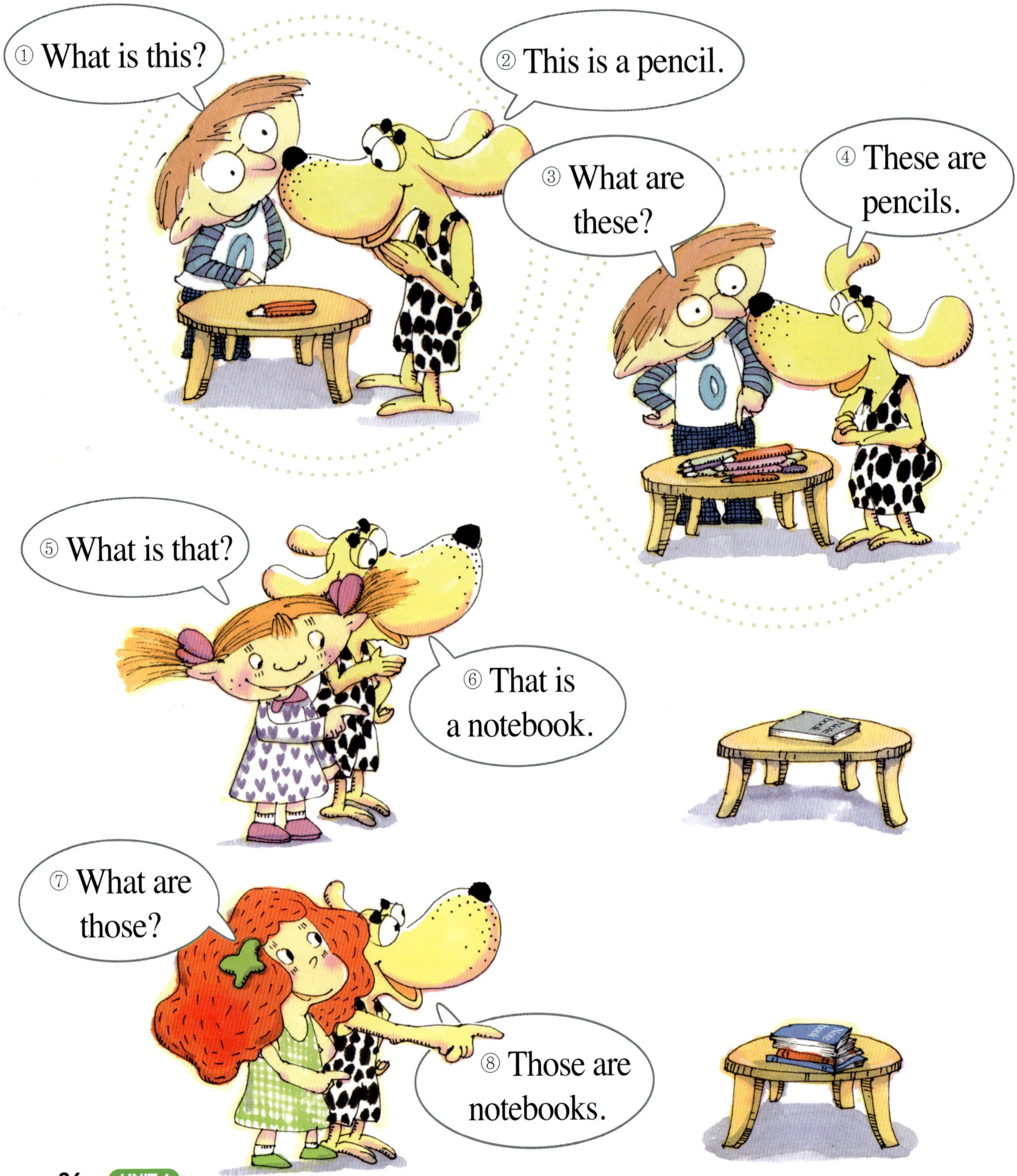

⑨ What is this?
⑩ This is a chair.

⑪ What is that?
⑫ That is a vase.

⑬ What is that?
⑭ That is a television.

dog

doll

desk

door

duck

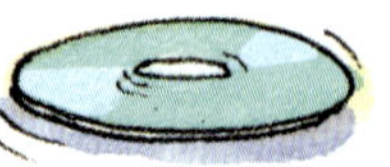

disk

Let's play

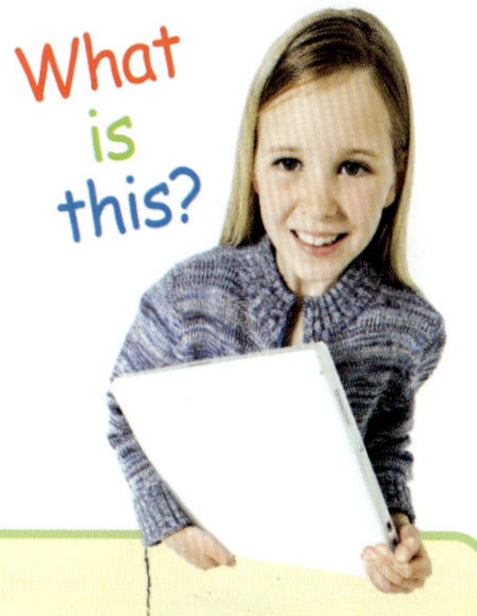

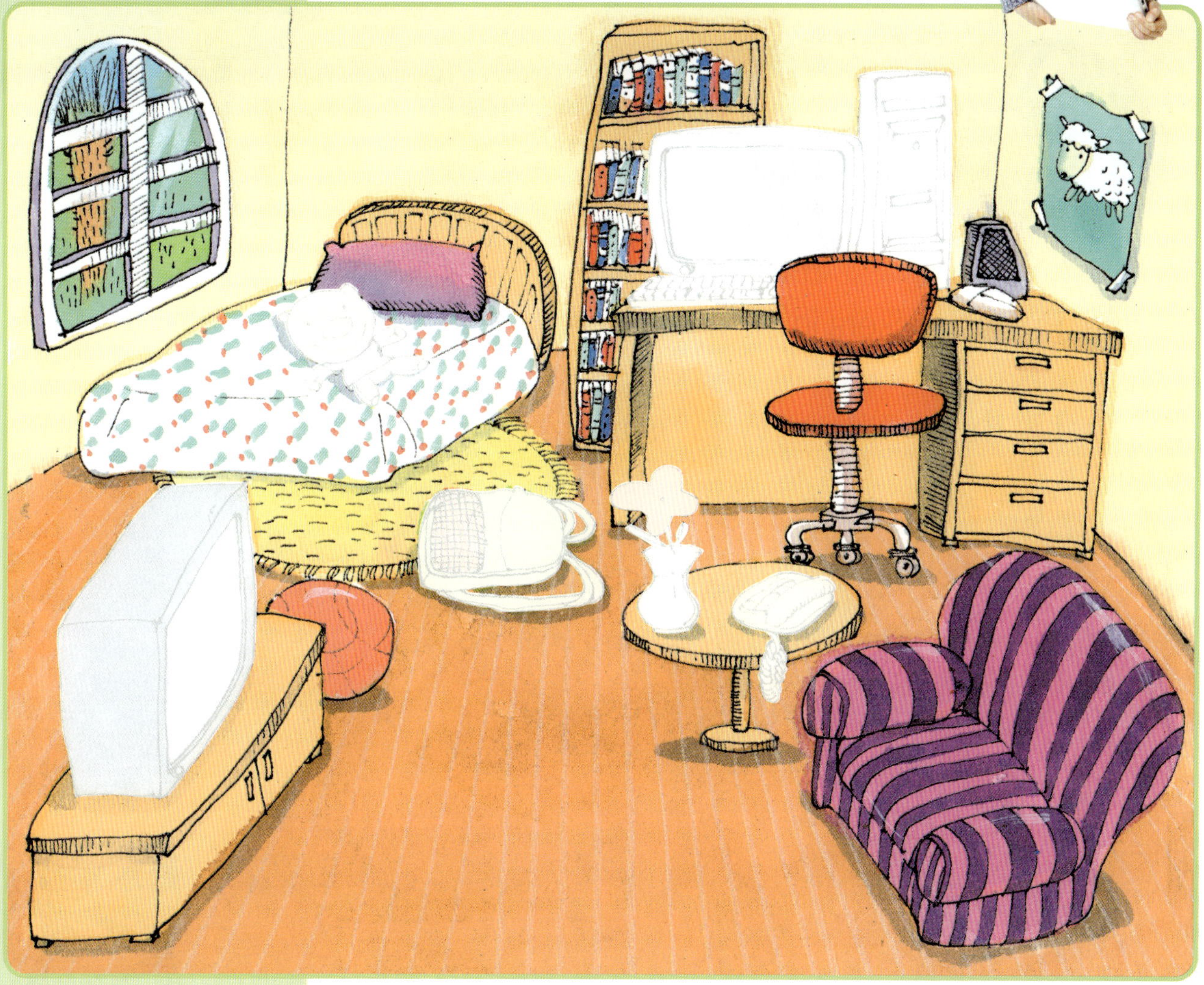

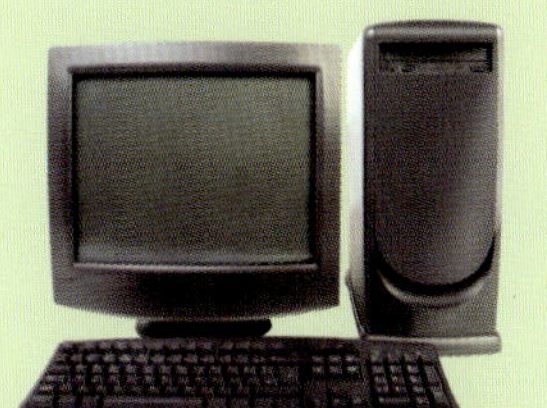

computer

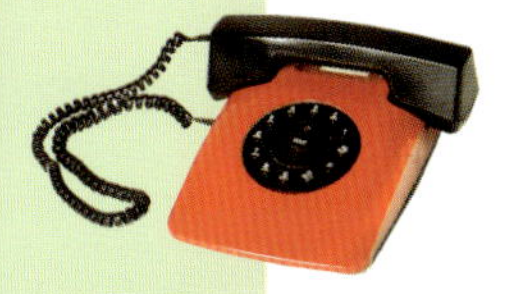

telephone

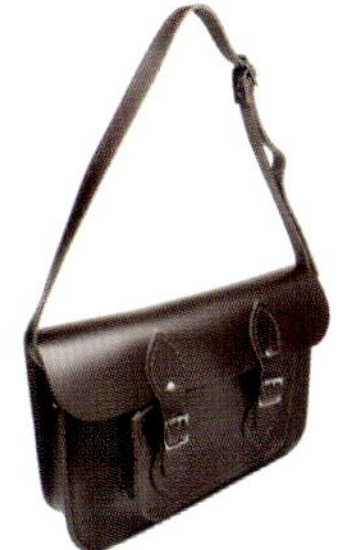

bag

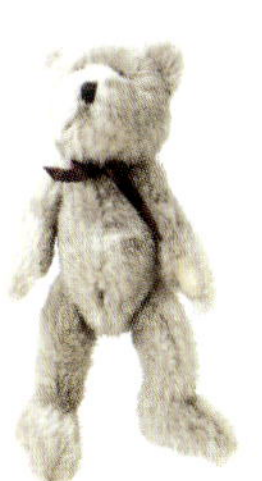

doll

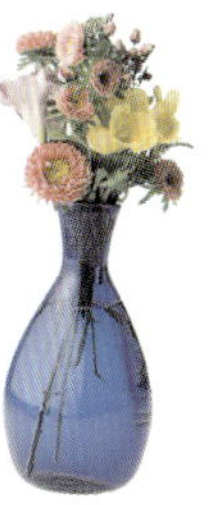

vase

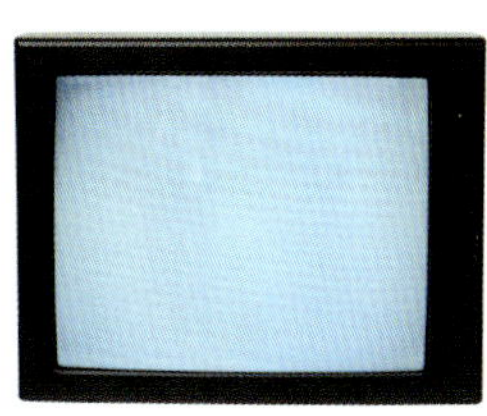

television

Put the stickers in the right place. Then, say
"What is this? This is a ________."

  ## Let's practice

A Listen and number.  **22**

B Listen. Put the stickers in the right place.  **23**

❶ What is this?   **❷ What is that?**   **❸ What is that?**

That is
a

This is
a

That is
a

C Listen and number.  **24**

   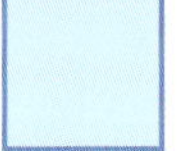

Let's sing

25

CAP

What's this?

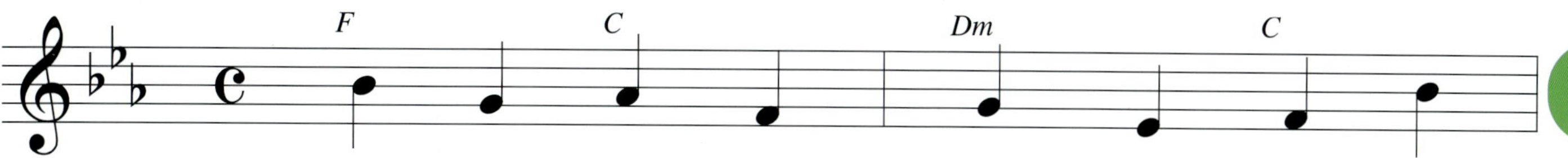

F   C   Dm   C
1. What's this? What's this?   What's   this?   What? What?
2. What's that? What's that?   What's   that?   What? What?

F   Gm   C   F
It's   a   cap. It's   a   cap.   It's   a   cap, cap, cap.
It's   a   bag. It's   a   bag.   It's   a   bag, bag, bag.

What's this?
What's this?

UNIT 5

Is it a book?

 Is it a book?

 Yes, it is.

 Is it a bus?

 No, it isn't. It's a taxi.

Listen and repeat

⑤ Is it a desk?
⑥ Yes, it is.

⑦ Is it an apple?
⑧ No, it isn't. It's a pear.

⑨ Is it a notebook?
⑩ Yes, it is.

F f

fish

fat

fox

fan

fly

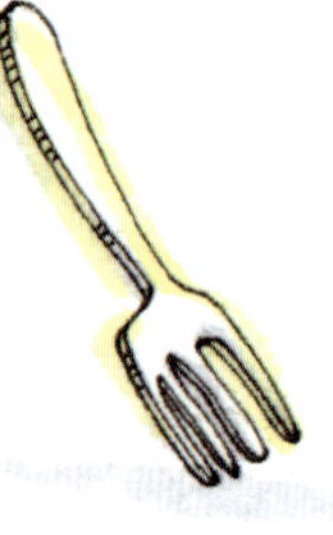

fork

Let's play

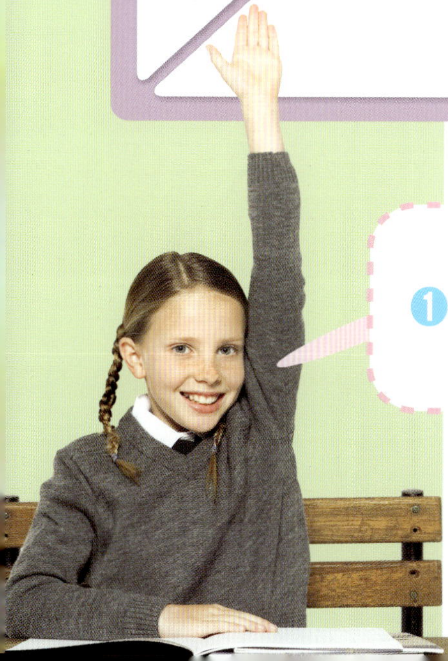

What's missing?

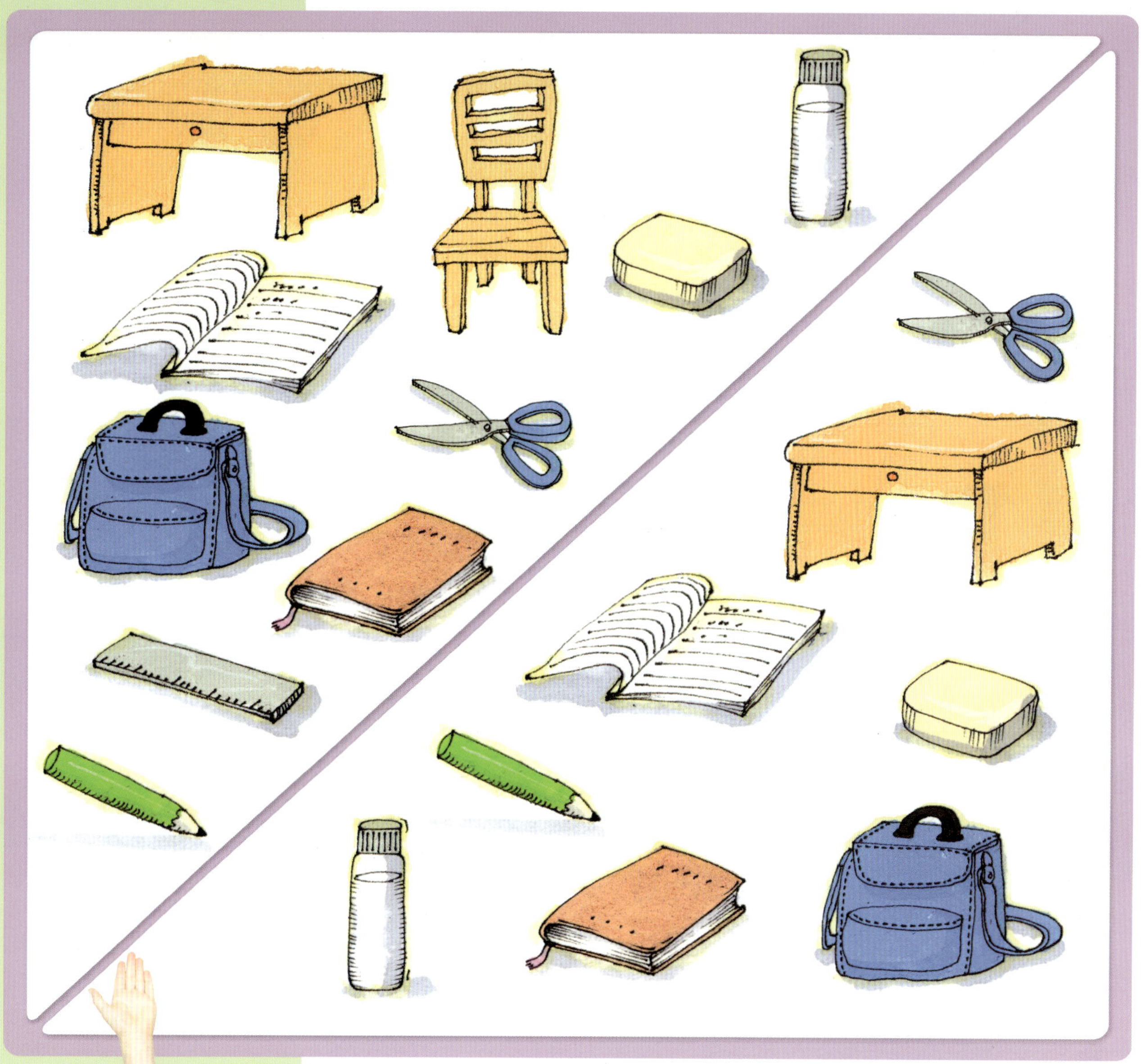

 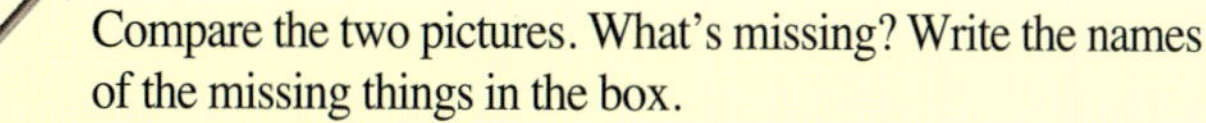

 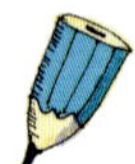 ## Let's practice

A Listen. Write O or X. 

①  ②  ③ 

B Write the correct word in the blanks.

① 

Is it a __________?
Yes, it is.

② 

Is it a chair?
No, it isn't.
It's a __________.

③ 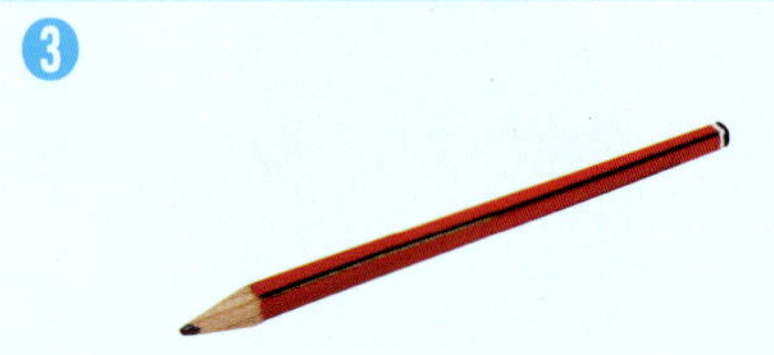

Is it a __________?
Yes, it is.

C Listen and number. 

   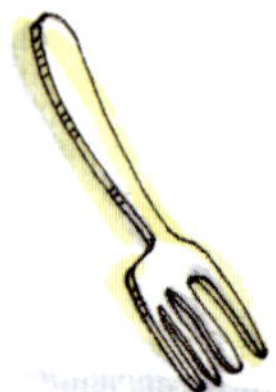

At school

book

desk

chair

notebook

pencil

eraser

ruler

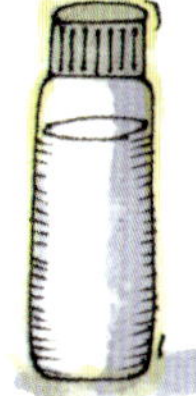

glue

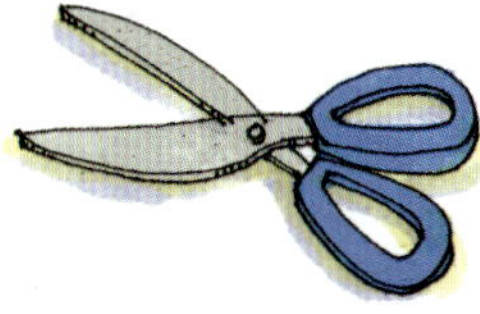

scissors

What's this?

UNIT 6

Who is he?

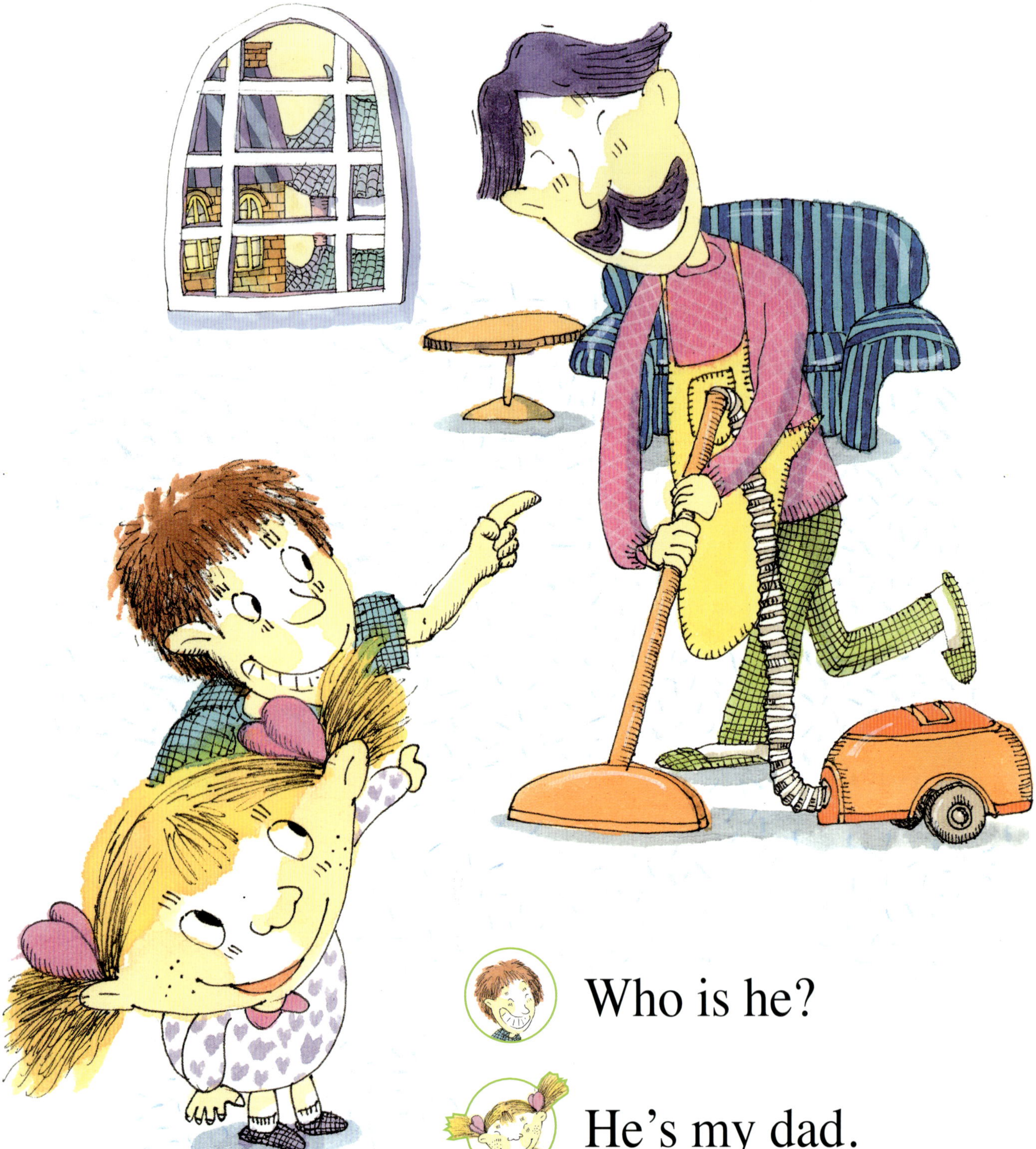

Who is he?

He's my dad.

6

Listen and repeat
33

grandfather
grandmother
② He is my
________ .
① Who is he?
④ She is my
________ .
③ Who is she?

father
father
mother
mother
sister
brother
cousin
baby sister

van

vest

violin

vet

vase

vine

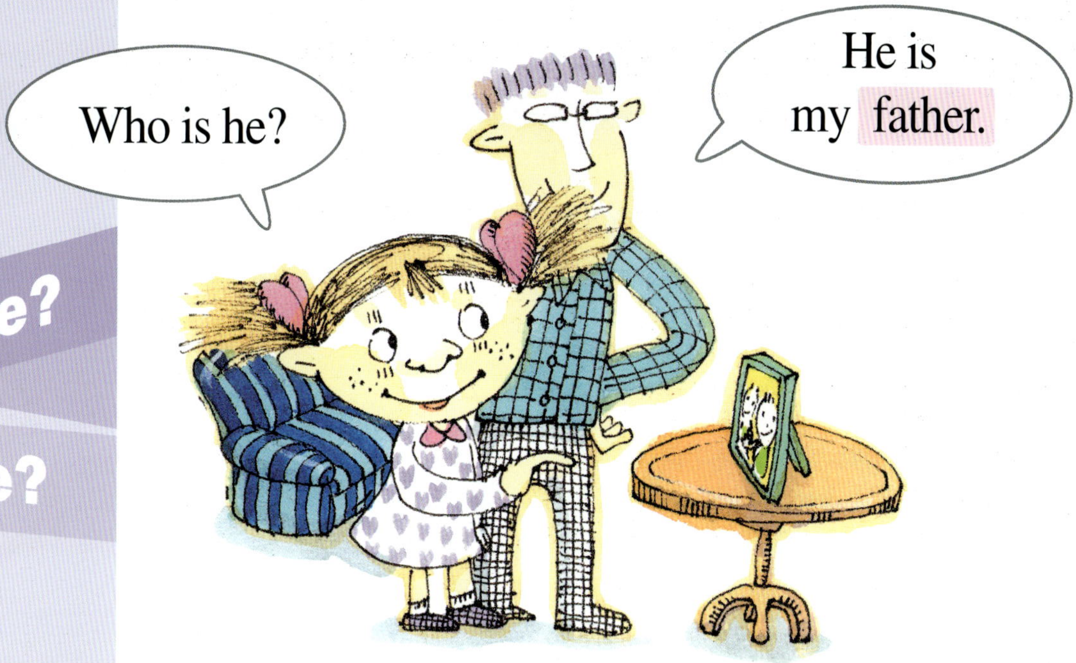

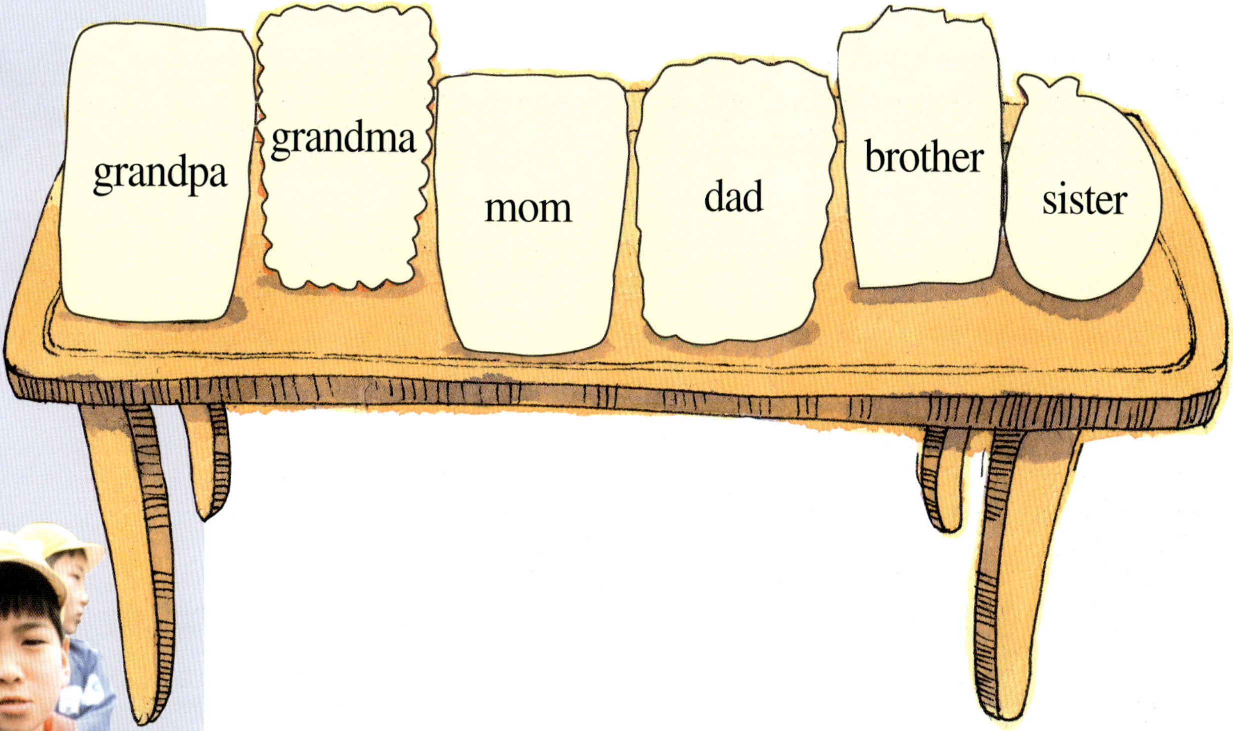

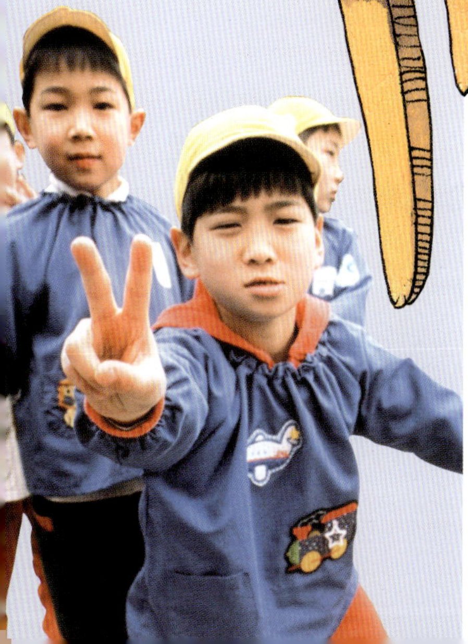

Put the stickers in the right place. Make a family album.
After that, ask "Who is she?" "She is ______." with a partner.

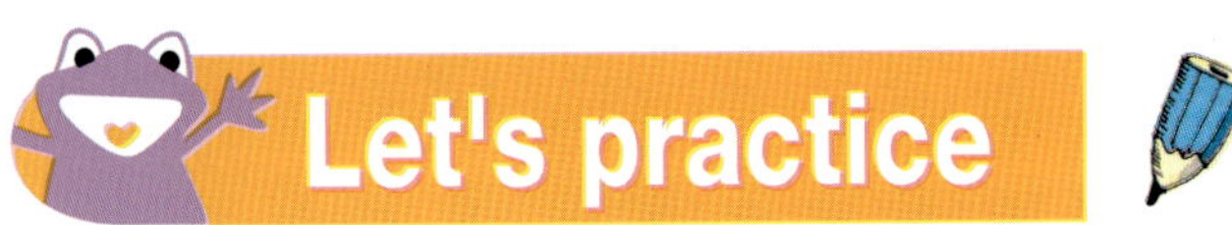Let's practice

 Listen and match. 

 ❶    ❷    ❸

 Write the correct word.

 ❶    ❷    ❸    ❹ 

 Listen and number. 

Happy home

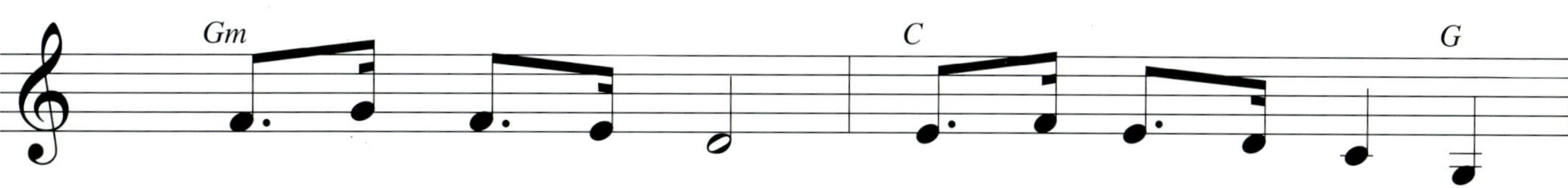

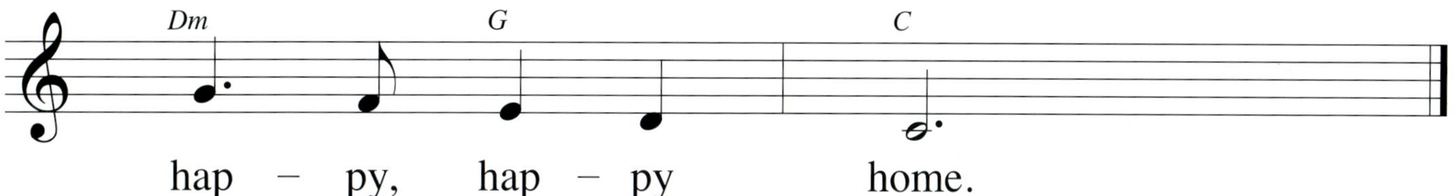

2. mother
3. brother
4. sister

UNIT 7 — What color is it?

Look! What color is it?

It's blue.

7

 What color is it?

 It's yellow!

Listen and repeat

39

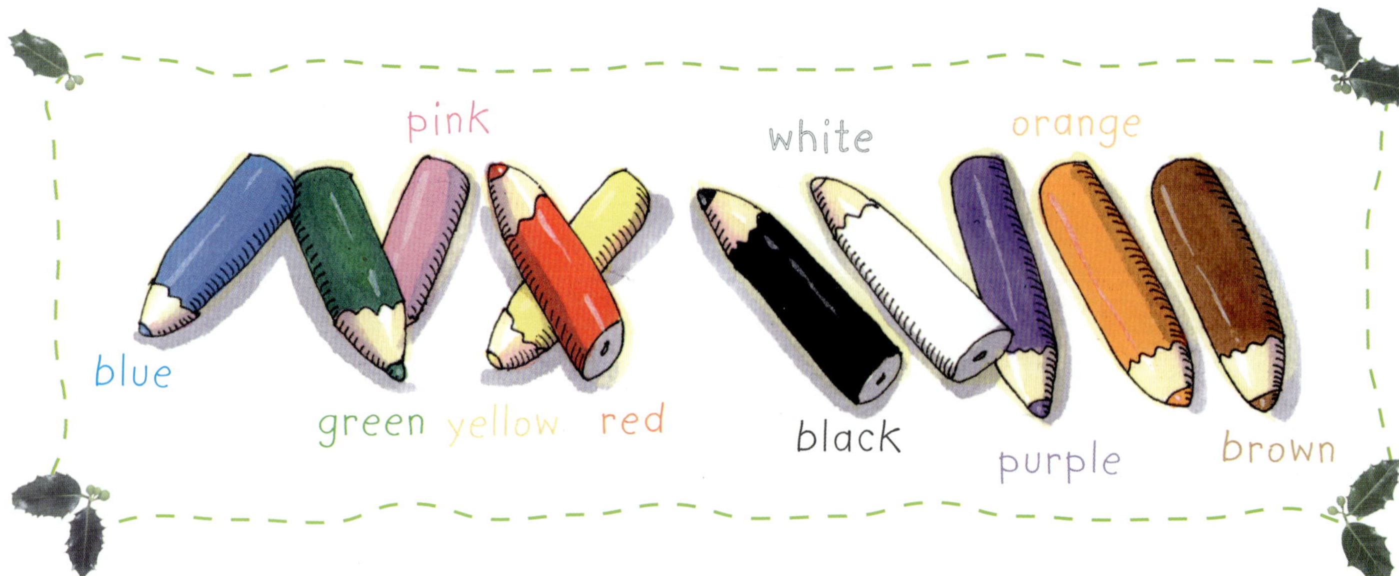

⑤ What color is it?
⑥ It's pink.

⑦ What color is it?
⑧ It's black.

⑨ What color is it?
⑩ Oh, it's white!

six

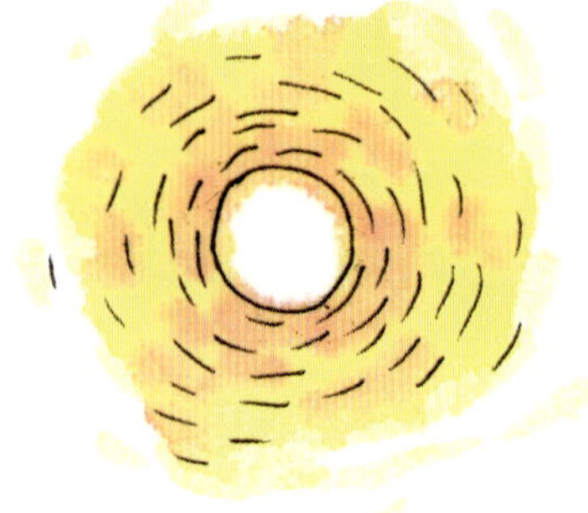

sun

sand

star

sit

swim

Let's play

Color the picture!

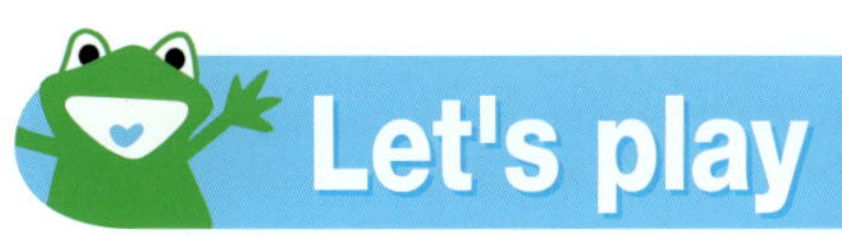

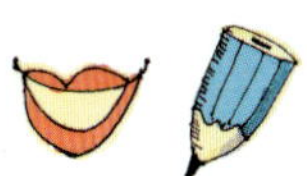

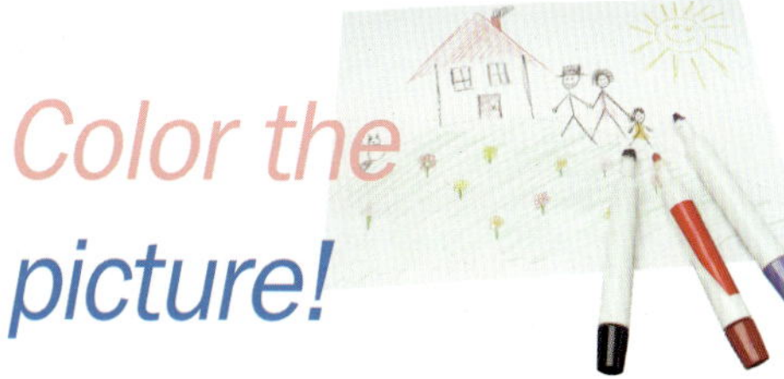

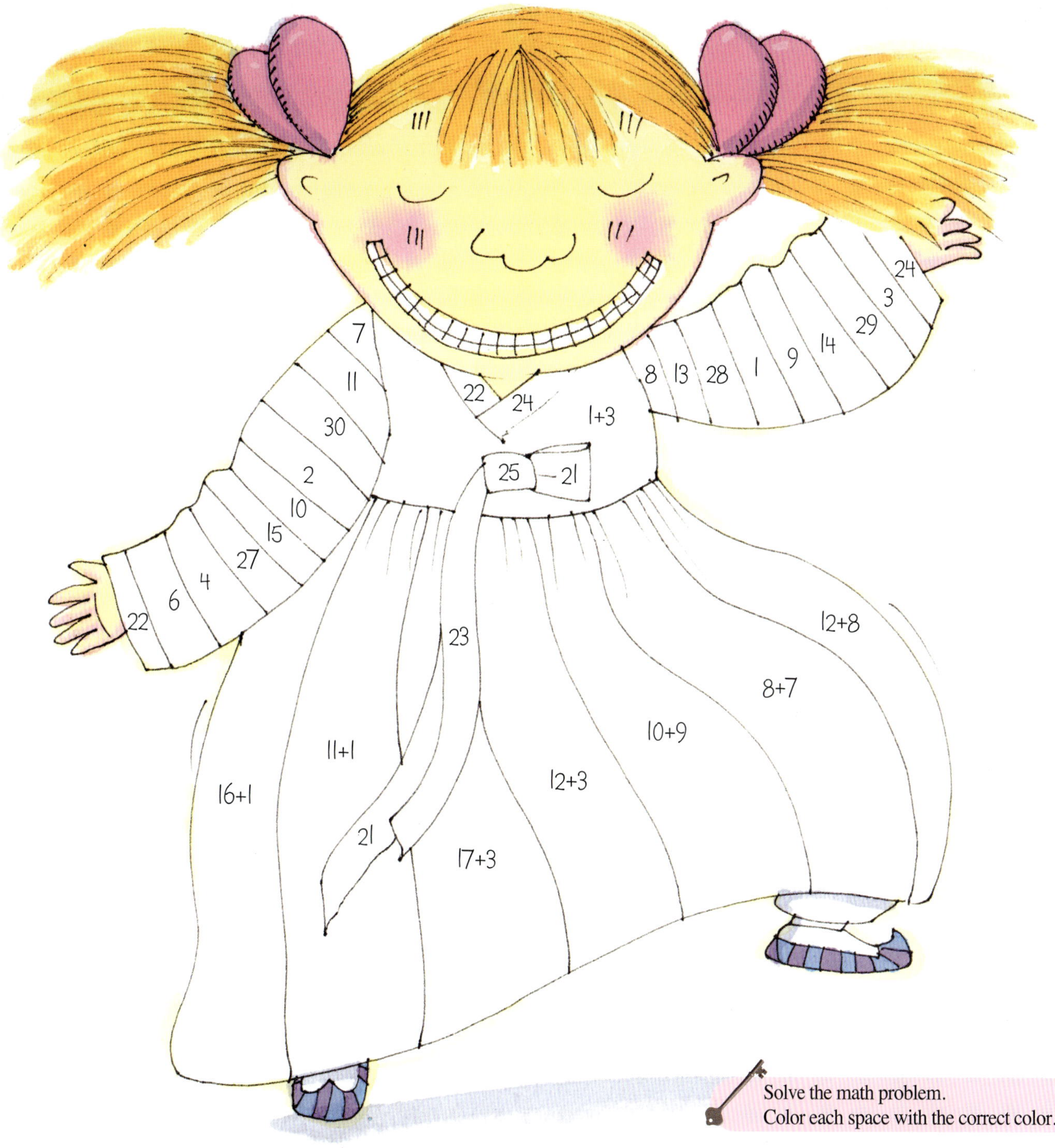

Solve the math problem.
Color each space with the correct color.

1 ~ 5	= yellow	11 ~ 15	= green	21 ~ 25	= blue
6 ~ 10	= red	16 ~ 20	= pink	26 ~ 30	= orange

Let's practice

A Listen. Put the stickers in the right place. 

❶   ❷    ❸    ❹ 

B Draw lines from the words to the correct flags.

❶    ❷    ❸    ❹ 

white   blue   orange   pink

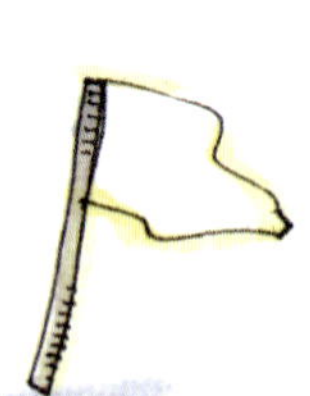  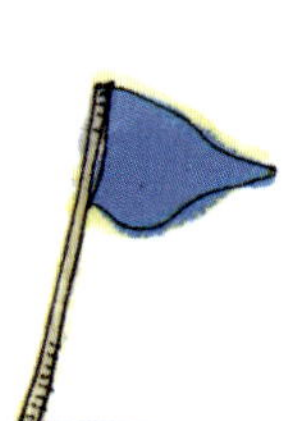 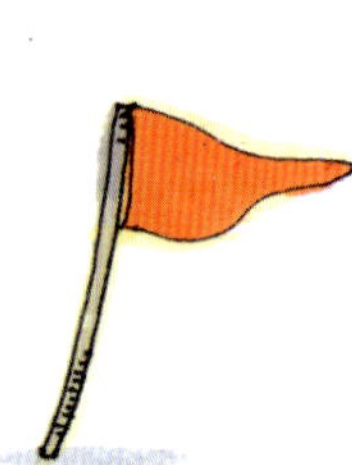

C Listen and number. 

 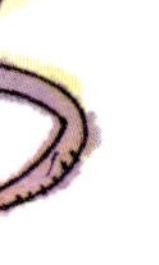   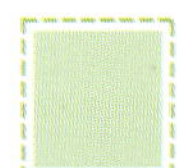   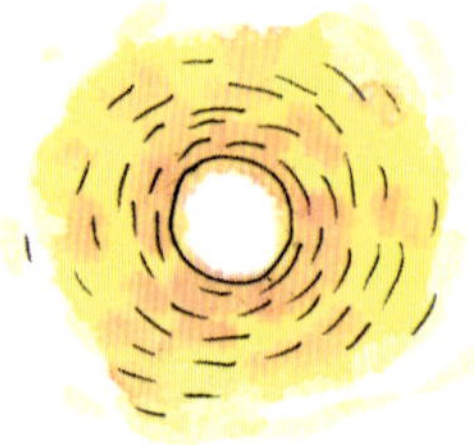 

Color

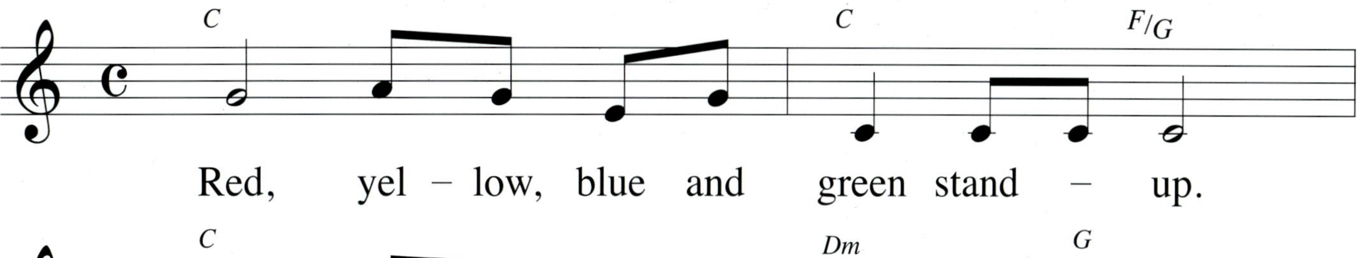
C
C
F/G
Red,   yel – low, blue and   green stand   –   up.

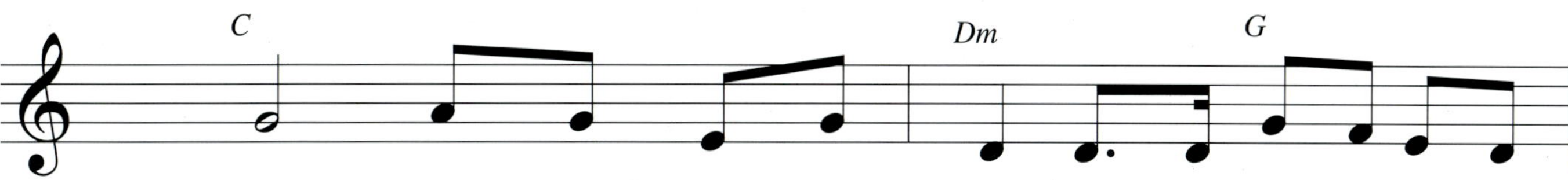
C
Dm
G
Red,   yel – low, blue and   green turn   a – round, and –

7

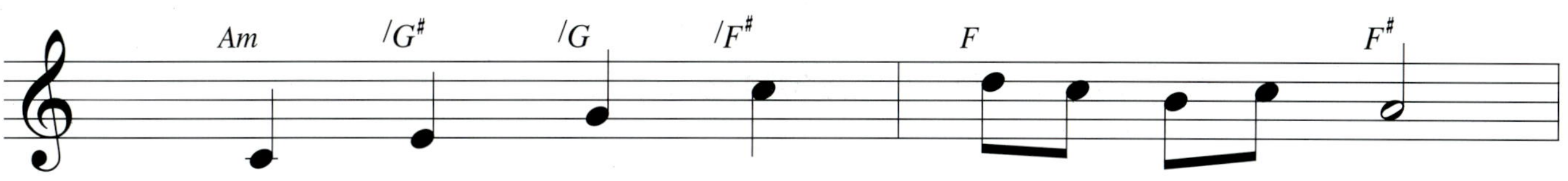
Am   /G#   /G   /F#   F   F#
stretch   up   high   a –   bove   your   head.

G   C G C
Red,   yel – low, blue and   green   sit down.

What do you like?

I like ice cream.

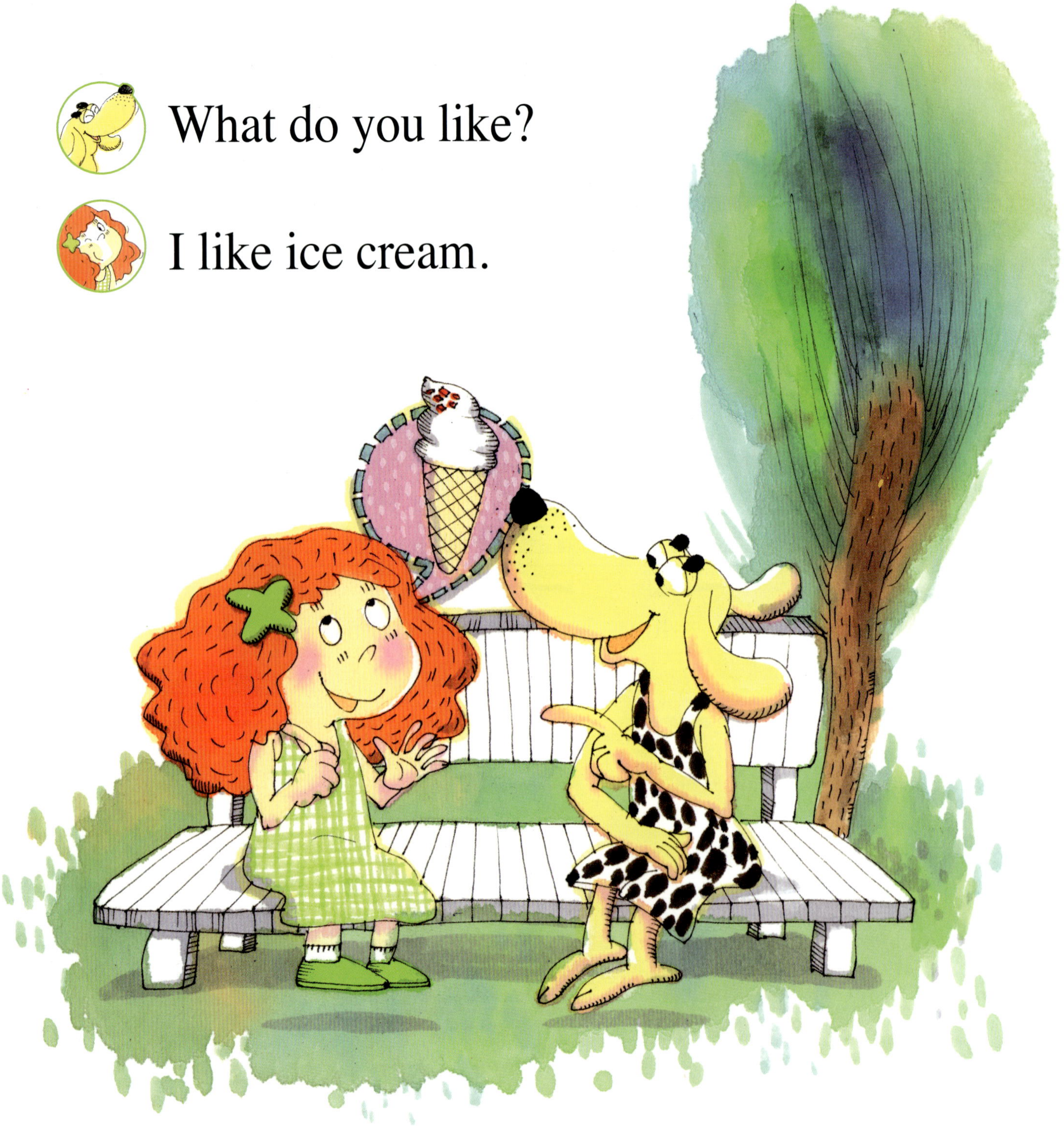

What do you like?

I like hamburgers.

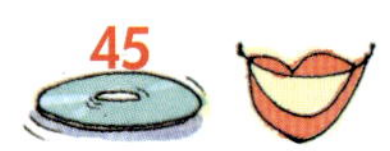

① What do you like?
② I like pizza.

③ What do you like?
④ I like chicken.

⑤ What do you like?
⑥ I like milk.
⑦ I like cake.
⑧ I like cookies!
I like candies. 
I like candies.

46

Z z

zebra

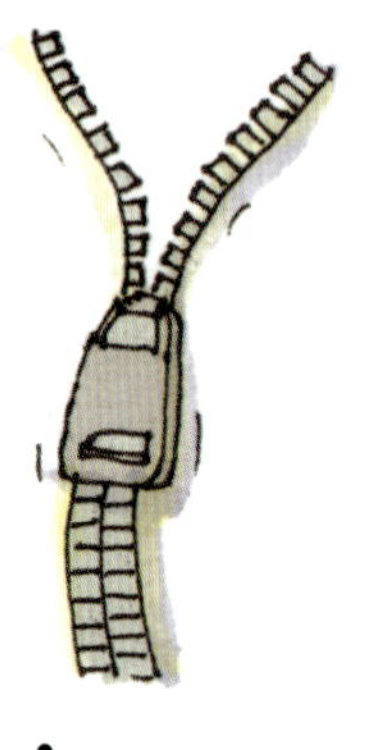

zipper

zoo

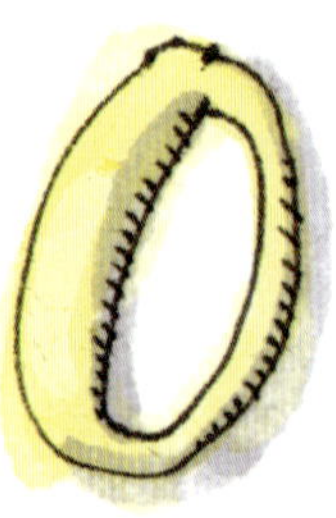

zero

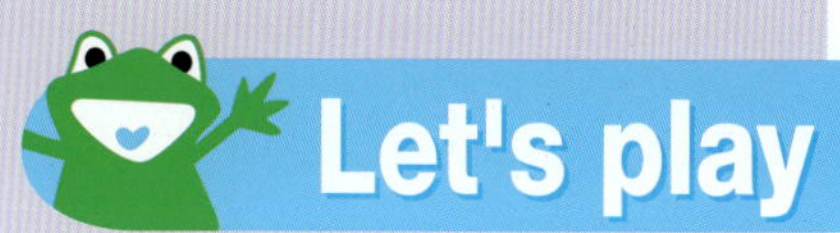

Color the triangles!

8

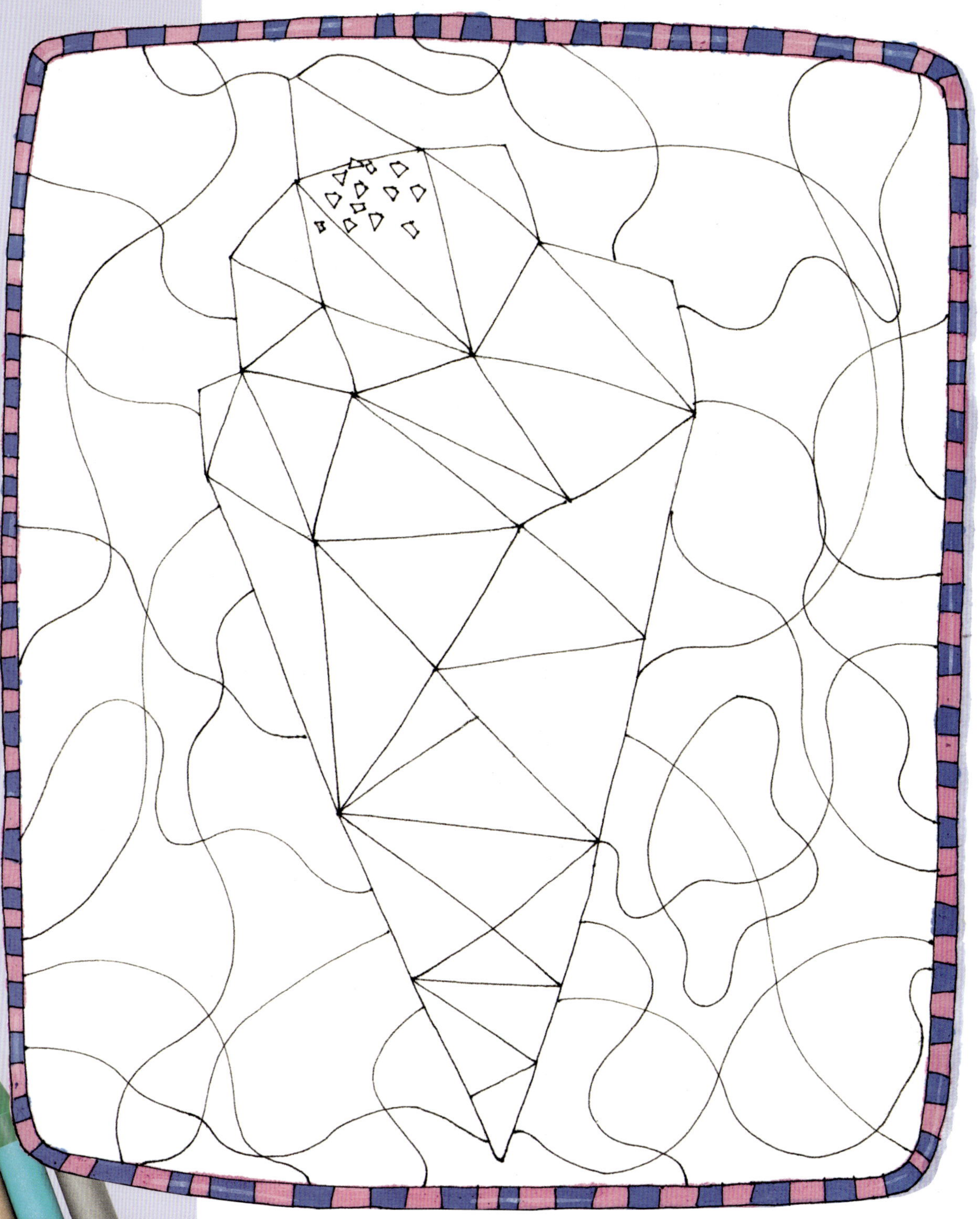

Color the triangles in the picture. What is it?

Let's practice

A Listen and number.  47

    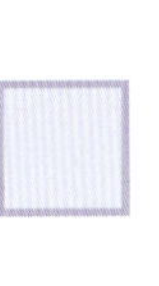   

B Work with a partner. Ask and answer.

C Listen and number.  48

      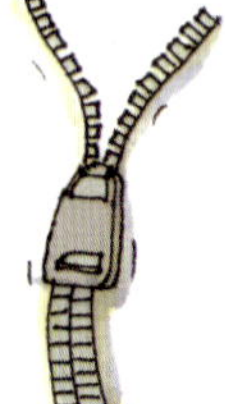   

I like ice cream

* lollipops

Do you like oranges?

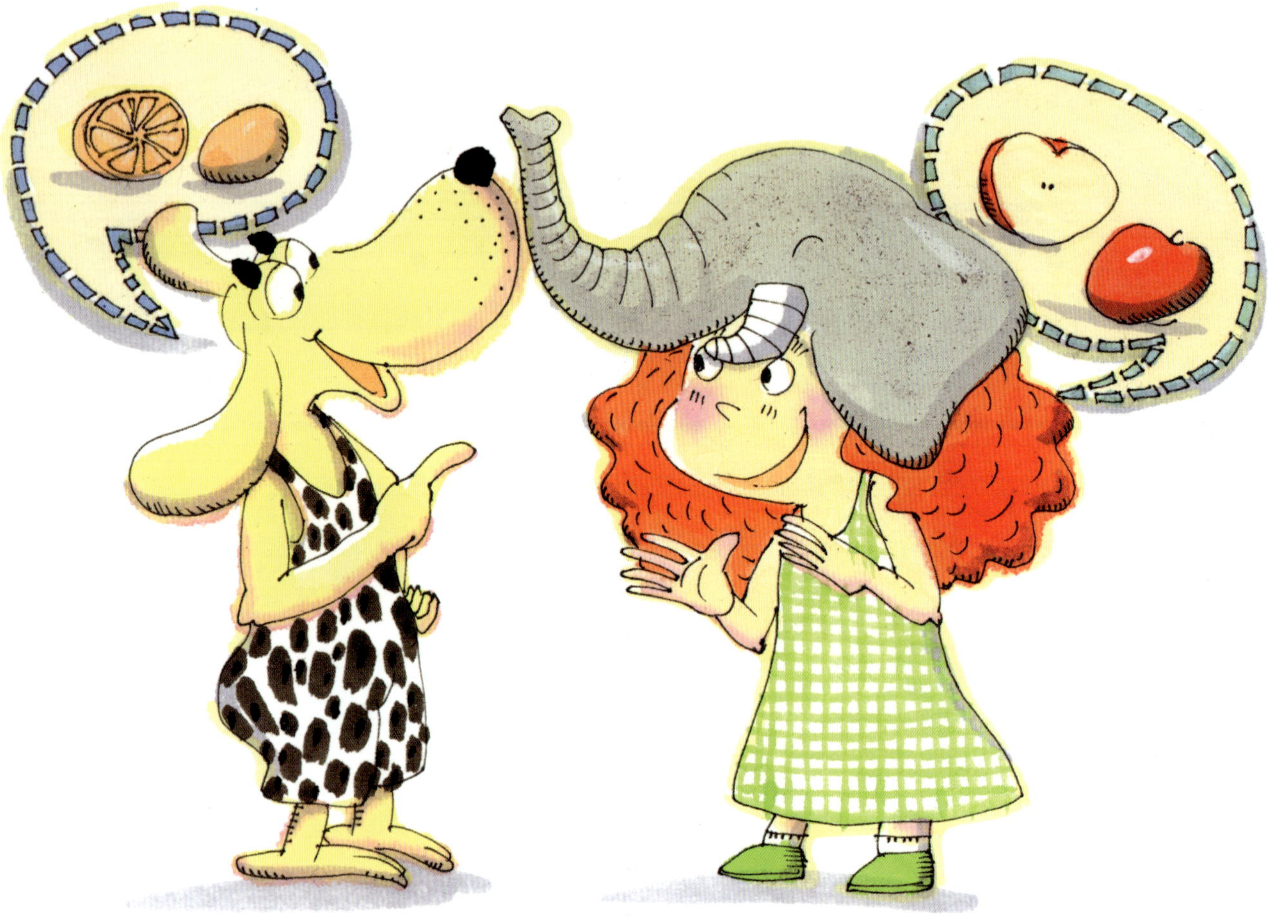

 Do you like oranges?

 No, I don't. I like apples.

9

 Do you like bananas?

 Yes, I do.

 ## Listen and repeat  51

bananas

kiwis

watermelon

9

pineapples

strawberries

 52 

  **C c**  

cat

car

cake

  **K k**  

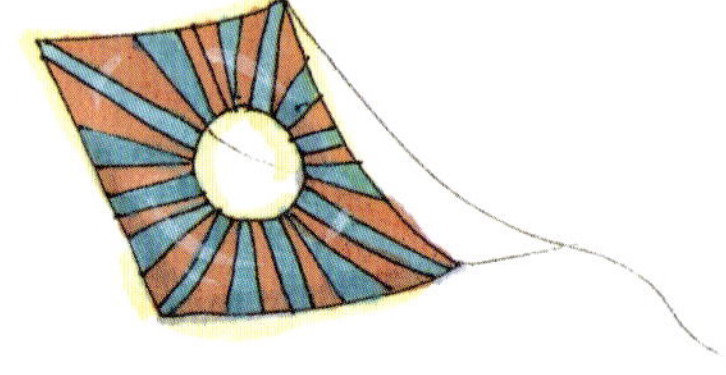

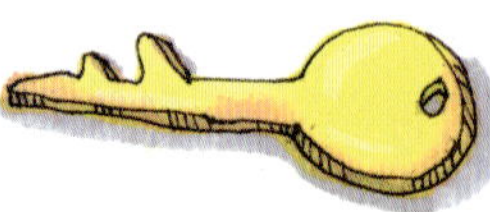

king

kite

key

At the market

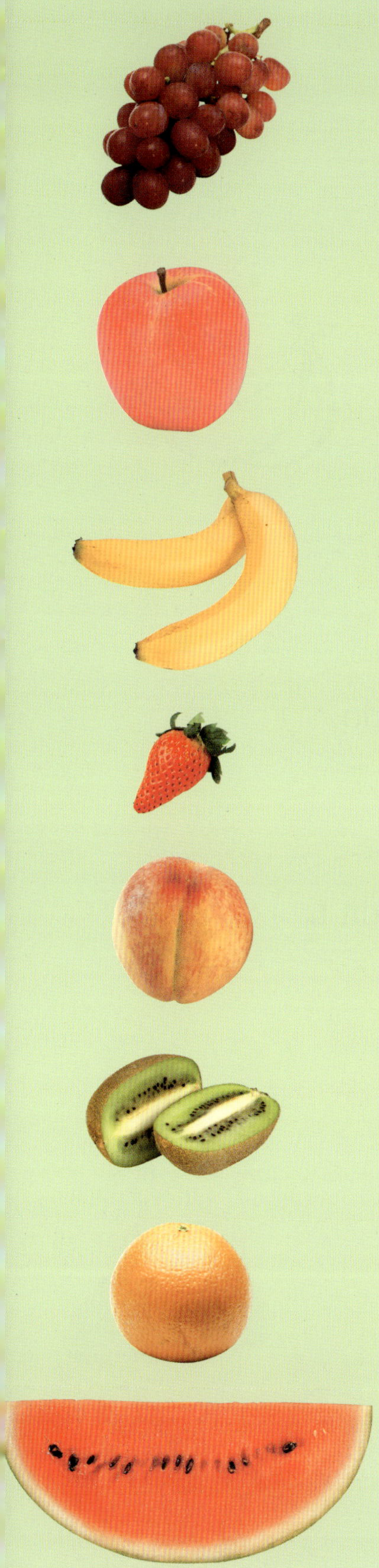

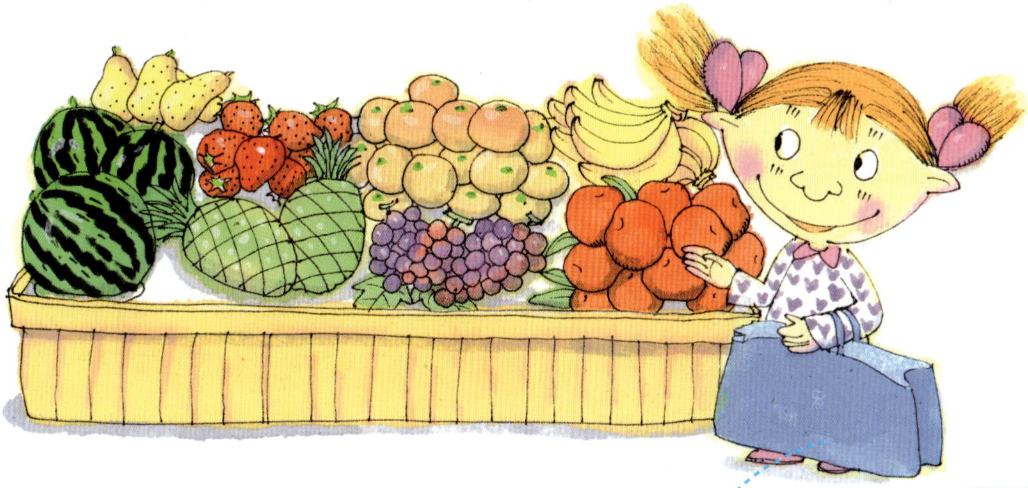

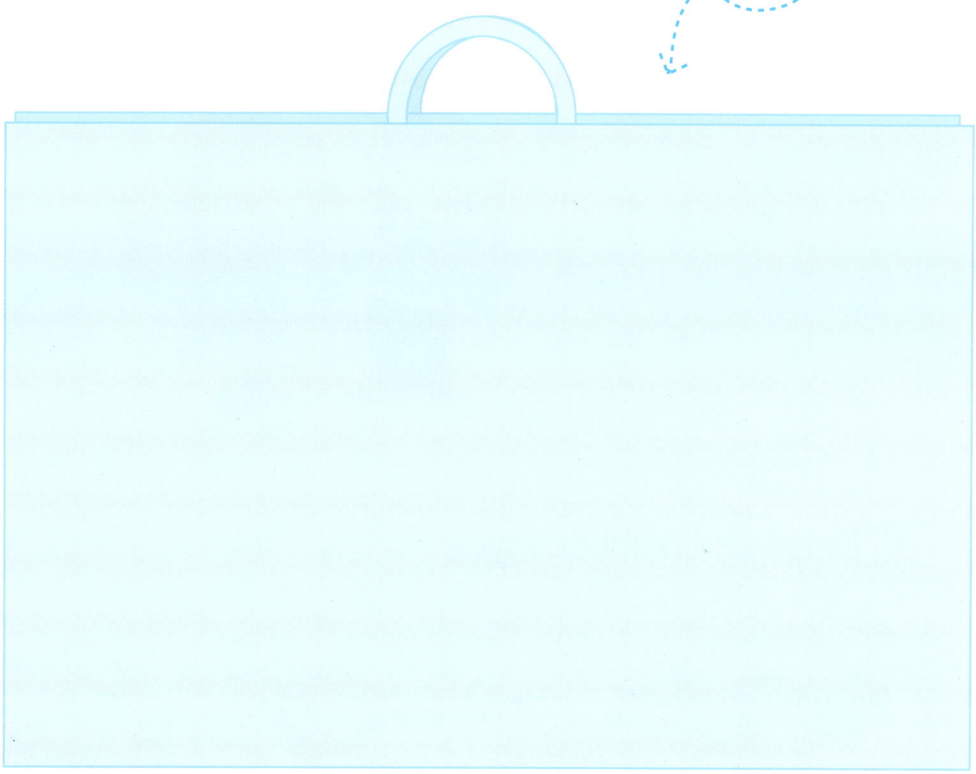

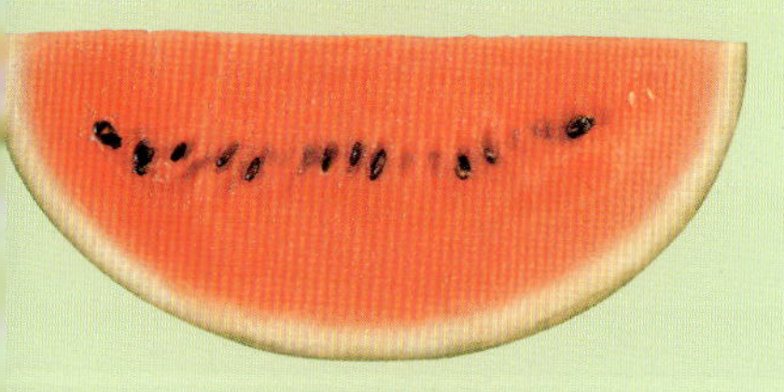

Choose your favorite fruits. Put the stickers in the box.
Ask and answer "Do you like ________?"

  # Let's practice 

A Listen and match. 53

❶　　　　　❷　　　　　❸

B Work with a partner. Ask and answer.

C Listen and number. 54 

 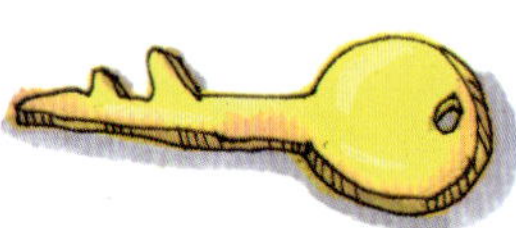  

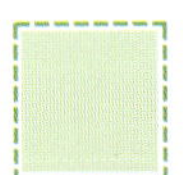  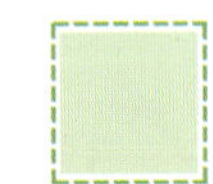 

Food

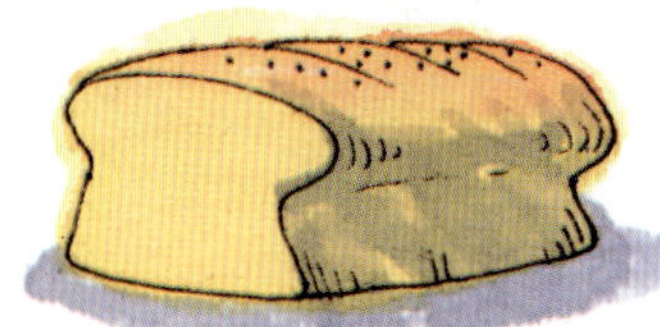

bread

hot dogs

cookies

cheese

salad

rice

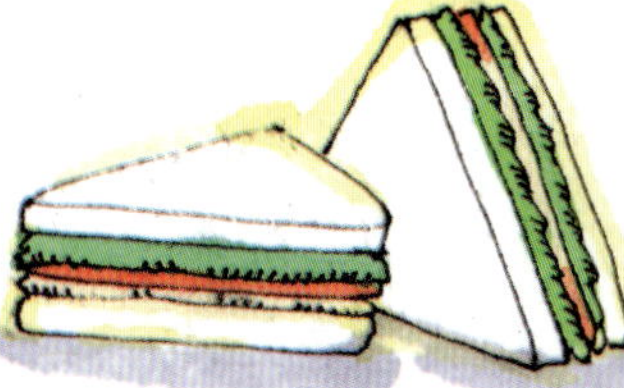

sandwiches

sausage

9

UNIT 10 How old are you?

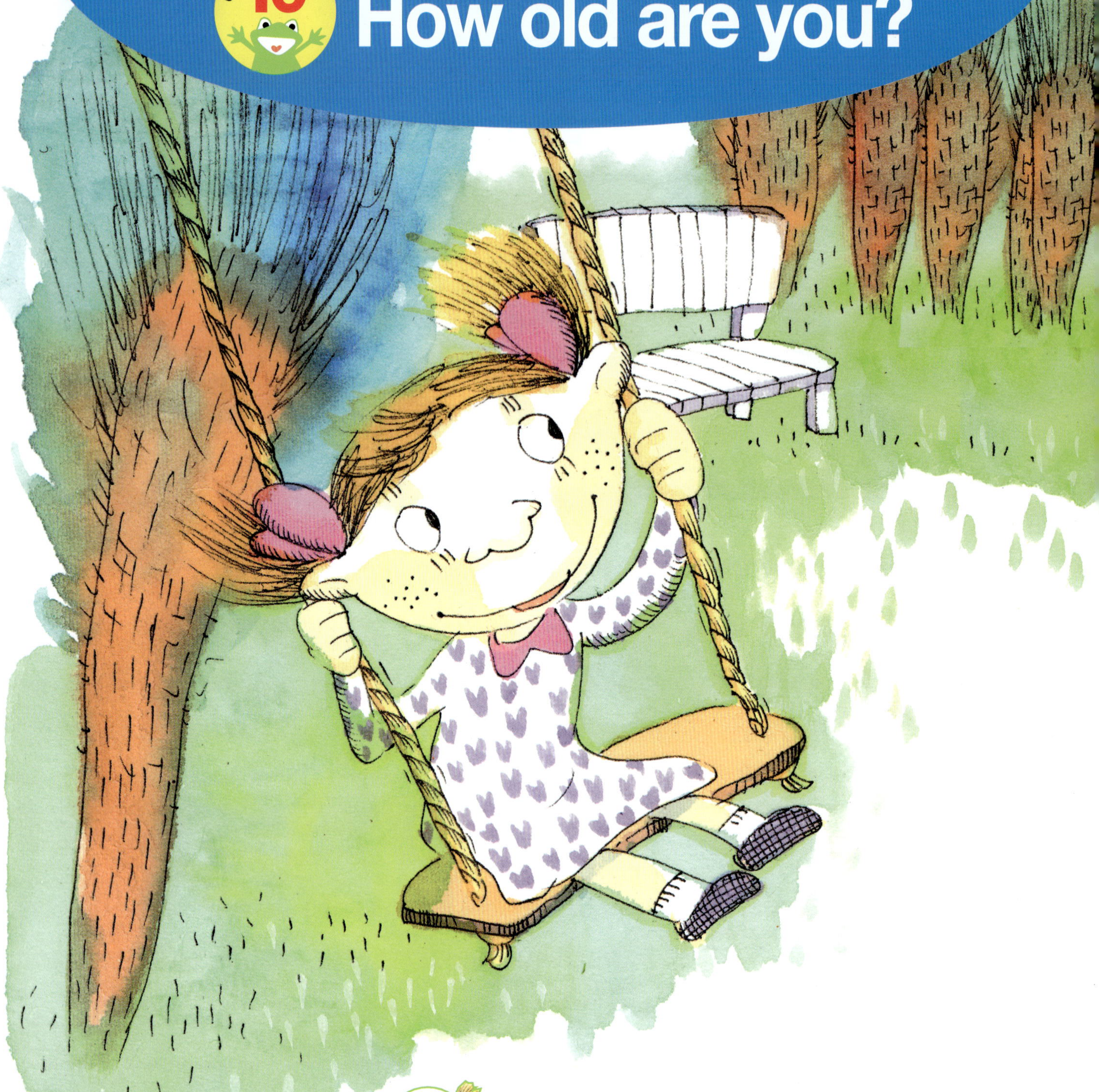

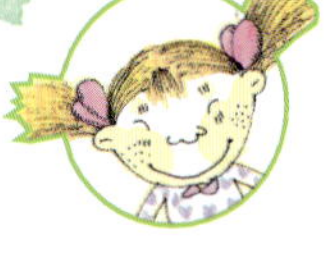

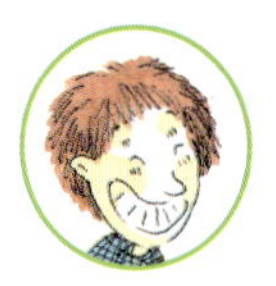

How old are you?

I'm seven years old.

 How old is he?

He is six years old.

one
two
three
four
five
six
seven
eight
nine
ten

① How old are you?
② I'm five.

③ How old are you?
④ I'm nine years old.

10

⑤ How old are you?
⑥ I'm four.

Tip
다음과 같이 묻고 답해 보세요.
How old is she?
She is _____ years old.
How old is he?
He is _____ years old.

G g

game

goat

girl

gate

gum

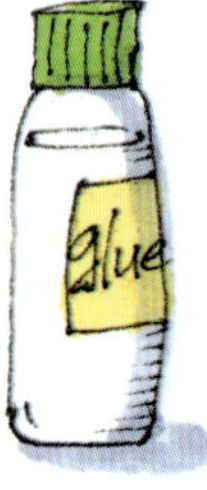

glue

Let's play

How old are you?
I'm _______ years old.

Hold your pencil over
the middle of the circle.

Let go.

Draw the candles
on the birthday cake.

Work with a partner. Ask and
answer "How old are you?"
"I'm _______ years old."

1. I'm _______.   2. I'm _______.   3. I'm _______.

10

  **Let's practice**

A Listen and number. **59**

B Write the correct word.

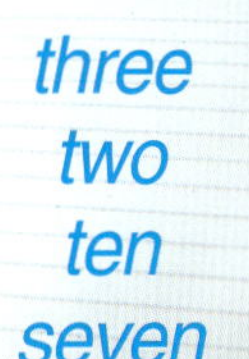

1 

2 

3 

4 

C Listen and number. **60**

Ten little puppies

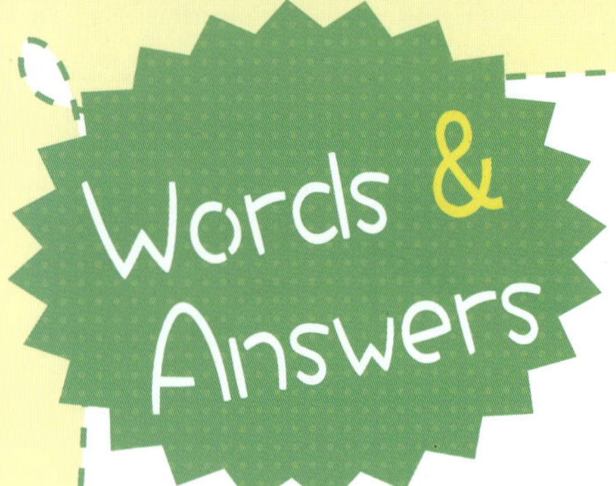

Words & Answers

■ Words

hello	안녕(만났을 때 인사말)
hi	안녕(만났을 때 인사말)
goodbye	잘 가(헤어질 때 인사말)
bye	잘 가(헤어질 때 인사말)
Hannah	한나(이름)
Joshua	조슈아(이름)
Ethan	이튼(이름)
Olivia	올리비아(이름)
Dusty	더스티(이름)
Ms. Smith	스미스 선생님
everyone	여러분, 모두들
how	어떻게
are	~이다(2인칭 복수)
you	너, 너희
I'm = I am	
I	나
am	~이다(1인칭 단수)
fine	기분이 좋은
good	기분 좋은
this	이것, 이 사람
is	~이다(3인칭 단수)

■ Phonics - P

pencil	연필
puppy	강아지
pan	후라이팬
pig	돼지
pins	핀
pot	냄비

■ Dialogue

안녕, 조슈아!

안녕, 한나!

잘 가!

잘 가!

■ Listen and repeat

① 안녕하세요, 스미스 선생님!

② 안녕, 한나!

③ 안녕, 얘들아!

④ 어떻게 지내?

⑤ 난 좋아.

⑥ 난 잘 지내.

⑦ 한나, 얘는 조슈아야.

⑧ 안녕, 조슈아!

⑨ 안녕, 한나!

⑩ 잘 가!

⑪ 잘 가!

■ Let's practice

A.

2　　1　　3

B.

❶

❷

C.

3   1   4   2

■ Let's sing

♪ 안녕

안녕, 안녕, 안녕. 어떻게 지내?
난 좋아, 난 좋아. 너도 그러길 바래.
안녕, 안녕, 안녕. 어떻게 지내?
난 좋아, 난 좋아. 너도 그러길 바래.

UNIT2   Thank you!

■ Words

Thank you!	고마워!
You're welcome!	천만에!
I'm sorry!	미안해!
That's all right!	괜찮아!
okay	괜찮은
that	저, 그
that's = that is	
you're = you are	

■ Phonics - B

book	책
ball	공
bed	침대
bus	버스
bag	가방
bike	자전거

■ Dialogue

 고마워!

 천만에!

 미안해!

 괜찮아!

■ Listen and repeat

① 고마워요!
② 천만에요!
③ 미안합니다!
④ 괜찮아요!
⑤ 고마워!
⑥ 천만에!
⑦ 미안합니다!
⑧ 괜찮아요!
⑨ 고맙다!
⑩ 천만에요!
⑪ 미안해요!
⑫ 괜찮아!

■ Let's practice

A.

 2    1

B.

❶

❷

C.

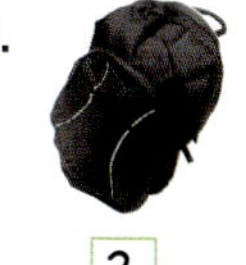   

2   1   3   4

■ Let's sing

♪ 고마워

고마워, 고마워. 정말 고마워.
천만에, 천만에, 천만에.
미안, 미안, 미안해.
음, 괜찮아, 괜찮아.

UNIT3 — What is your name?

■Words

what	무엇
your	너의(you의 소유격)
name	이름
my	나의(I의 소유격)
what's = what is	
Jacob	제이콥(이름)

■Phonics - T

tiger	호랑이
toy	장난감
ten	열(10)
top	팽이
tape	테이프
toe	발가락

■Dialogue

넌 이름이 뭐야?
내 이름은 조슈아야. 너는 이름이 뭐야?
난 한나야.
안녕, 한나!

■Listen and repeat

① 넌 이름이 뭐니?
② 난 올리비아야.
③ 안녕, 올리비아!
④ 안녕! 내 이름은 한나야.
⑤ 내 이름은 조슈아야.
⑥ 난 더스티야.
⑦ 안녕! 난 이튼이야.
⑧ 내 이름은 제이콥이야.

■Let's practice

A.

1 4 2 3

C.

2 1 4 3

■Let's sing

♪넌 이름이 뭐야?
안녕, 안녕. 내 이름은 한나야.
내 이름은 한나야. 넌 이름이 뭐야?
안녕, 안녕. 내 이름은 더스티야.
넌 이름이 뭐야?

UNIT4 — What is this?

■Words

this	이, 이것 (가까운 것을 가리킴)
a	하나의(부정관사)
bag	가방
that	저것, 그것 (먼 것을 가리킴)
cap	야구모자
pencil	연필
these	이것들(this의 복수형)
notebook	공책, 노트
those	저것들, 그것들 (that의 복수형)
chair	의자
vase	꽃병
television	텔레비전

Phonics - D

dog	개
doll	인형
desk	책상
door	문
duck	오리
disk	디스크

Dialogue

이건 뭐야?

이건 가방이야.

저건 뭐야?

저건 야구모자야.

Listen and repeat

① 이건 뭐야?
② 이건 연필이야.
③ 이것들은 뭐야?
④ 이것들은 연필이야.
⑤ 저건 뭐야?
⑥ 저건 공책이야.
⑦ 저것들은 뭐야?
⑧ 저것들은 공책이야.
⑨ 이건 뭐야?
⑩ 이건 의자야.
⑪ 저건 뭐야?
⑫ 저건 꽃병이야.
⑬ 저건 뭐야?
⑭ 저건 텔레비전이야.

Let's practice

A.

 2

 3

 1

B.

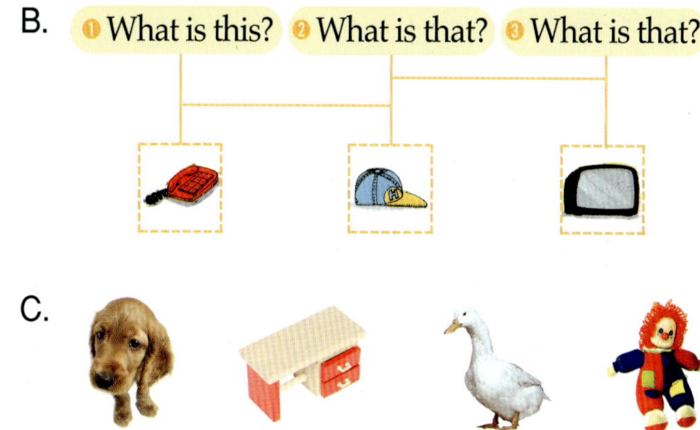

C.

4　　3　　1　　2

Let's sing

♪ 이건 뭐야?

1.
이건 뭐야? 이건 뭐야? 이건 뭐야? 뭐야? 뭐야?
그건 모자야. 그건 모자야. 그건 모자, 모자, 모자야.

2.
저건 뭐야? 저건 뭐야? 저건 뭐야? 뭐야? 뭐야?
그건 가방이야. 그건 가방이야. 그건 가방, 가방, 가방이야.

UNIT5　Is it a book?

Words

it	그것(무생물이나 성별이 분명하지 않을 때 씀)
book	책
yes	네(긍정을 나타냄)
bus	버스
no	아니오(부정을 나타냄)
isn't = is not	
it's = it is	
taxi	택시
cat	고양이
dog	개
desk	책상
apple	사과
pear	배

■ Phonics - F

fish	물고기
fat	뚱뚱한
fox	여우
fan	선풍기
fly	파리
fork	포크

■ Dialogue

 그거 책이야?
 응, 그래.
 그거 버스야?
 아니야. 그건 택시야.

■ Listen and repeat

① 그거 연필이야?
② 응, 그래.
③ 그거 고양이야?
④ 아니야. 그건 개야.
⑤ 그거 책상이야?
⑥ 응, 그래.
⑦ 그거 사과야?
⑧ 아니야. 그건 배야.
⑨ 그거 공책이야?
⑩ 응, 그래.

■ Let's practice

A.
❶  ❷  ❸ 
  ×   ○   ○

B.
❶
Is it a <u>cat</u>?
Yes, it is.

❷
Is it a chair?

No, it isn't.
It's a <u>desk</u>.
❸
Is it a <u>pencil</u>?
Yes, it is.

C.    
  1   3   2   4

■ Let's learn more

At school — 학교에서

book	책
desk	책상
chair	의자
notebook	공책, 노트
pencil	연필
eraser	지우개
ruler	자
glue	풀
scissors	가위

UNIT6 Who is he?

■ Words

who	누구
he	그는(남자를 가리킴)
dad	아빠
they	그들은
mom	엄마
sister	여자형제
grandfather	할아버지
grandmother	할머니
she	그녀는(여자를 가리킴)
father	아버지
mother	어머니

brother	남자형제
cousin	사촌
baby sister	여동생

■Phonics - V

van	밴
vest	조끼
violin	바이올린
vet	수의사
vase	꽃병
vine	포도나무

■Dialogue

 그는 누구니?

그는 나의 아빠야.

 그들은 누구니?

그들은 나의 엄마와 나의 언니야.

■Listen and repeat

① 그는 누구니?
② 그는 나의 _______ 야.
③ 그녀는 누구니?
④ 그녀는 나의 _______ 야.

■Let's practice

A.

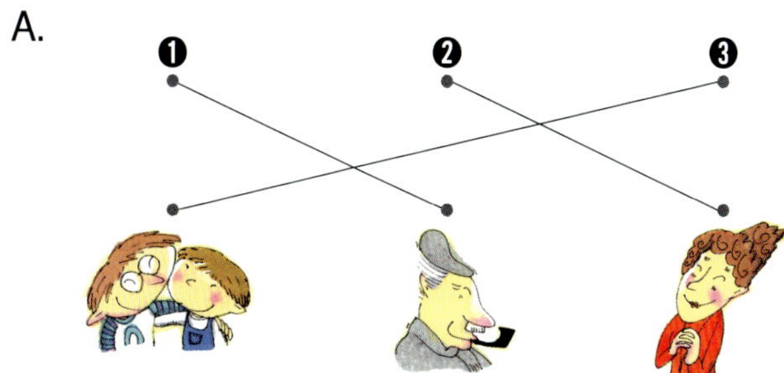

B.

❶ grandmother
❷ baby sister
❸ sisters
❹ father

C.

■Let's sing

♪즐거운 우리집
아빠와 함께하는 우리 가족, 행복하고 행복한 우리집,
행복하고 행복한 우리집, 행복하고 행복한 우리집.
아빠와 함께하는 우리 가족, 행복하고 행복한 우리집,
행복하고 행복한 우리집.

✻ 2. 엄마   3. 오빠, 형(남동생)   4. 언니, 누나(여동생)

UNIT7 What color is it?

■Words

look	보다
color	색, 색깔
blue	파란색
yellow	노란색
green	녹색
pink	분홍색
red	빨간색
black	검은색
white	흰색
purple	보라색
orange	주황색
brown	갈색

■Phonics - S

six	여섯(6)
sun	해, 태양
sand	모래
star	별
sit	앉다
swim	수영하다

 봐봐! 무슨 색깔이야?

 그건 파란색이야.

 무슨 색깔이야?

 노란색이야!

■Listen and repeat

① 무슨 색깔이야?

② 빨강색이야.

③ 무슨 색깔이야?

④ 오, 그건 녹색이야!

⑤ 무슨 색깔이야?

⑥ 그건 분홍색이야.

⑦ 무슨 색깔이야?

⑧ 검은색이야.

⑨ 무슨 색깔이야?

⑩ 오, 그건 흰색이야!

■Let's practice

A.

❶ 　❷ 　❸ 　❹ 

B.

❶ white　❷ blue　❸ orange　❹ pink

C.

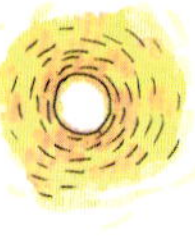			
2	3	4	1

■Let's sing

♪ 색깔

빨강, 노랑, 파랑 그리고 녹색은 일어서세요.

빨강, 노랑, 파랑 그리고 녹색은 돌아서세요, 그리고 손을 머리 위로 쭉 뻗으세요.

빨강, 노랑, 파랑 그리고 녹색은 앉으세요.

UNIT8　What do you like?

■Words

do	조동사
like	좋아하다
ice cream	아이스크림
hamburger	햄버거
pizza	피자
chicken	치킨
milk	우유
cake	케익
cookies	쿠키

■Phonics - Z

zebra	얼룩말
zipper	지퍼
zoo	동물원
zero	영(0)

■Dialogue

 넌 뭘 좋아하니?

 난 아이스크림을 좋아해.

 넌 뭘 좋아하니?

 난 햄버거를 좋아해.

■Listen and repeat

① 넌 뭘 좋아하니?

② 난 피자를 좋아해.

③ 넌 뭘 좋아하니?

④ 난 치킨을 좋아해.

⑤ 넌 뭘 좋아하니?

⑥ 난 우유를 좋아해.

⑦ 난 케익을 좋아해.
⑧ 난 쿠키가 좋아!

■Let's practice

A.

 2  3  1

C.

4   2   1   3

■Let's sing

♪난 아이스크림이 좋아

넌 뭘 좋아하니? 난 아이스크림을 좋아해.
너도 아이스크림 좋아하니? 응, 그래.
넌 뭘 좋아하니? 난 아이스크림을 좋아해.
나도 아이스크림을 좋아해.

＊ 막대사탕

UNIT9　Do you like oranges?

■Words

orange	오렌지
don't = do not	
apple	사과
banana	바나나
grape	포도
peach	복숭아
pear	배
watermelon	수박
kiwi	키위
pineapple	파인애플
strawberry	딸기

■Phonics - C & K

cat	고양이
car	자동차
cake	케익
king	왕
kite	연
key	열쇠

■Dialogue

너 오렌지 좋아해?

아니, 안 좋아해. 난 사과를 좋아해.

너 바나나 좋아해?

응, 그래.

■Listen and repeat

① 너 포도 좋아해?
② 응, 그래.
③ 너 복숭아 좋아해?
④ 아니, 안 좋아해.
⑤ 너 배 좋아해?
⑥ 아니, 안 좋아해.
⑦ 너 수박 좋아해?
⑧ 응, 그래!

■Let's practice

A.

❶　　❷　　❸

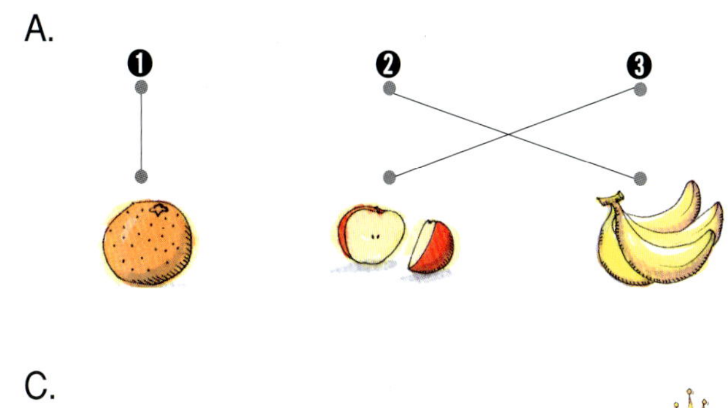

C.

1   4   3   2

■ Let's learn more

Food — 음식

bread	빵
hot dogs	핫도그
cookies	쿠키
cheese	치즈
salad	샐러드
rice	밥
sandwiches	샌드위치
sausage	소세지
french fries	감자튀김

UNIT10　How old are you?

■ Words

how	얼마나
old	나이 먹은, 늙은
year	연, 해
one	하나(1)
two	둘(2)
three	셋(3)
four	넷(4)
five	다섯(5)
six	여섯(6)
seven	일곱(7)
eight	여덟(8)
nine	아홉(9)
ten	열(10)

■ Phonics - G

game	게임
goat	염소
girl	소녀
gate	대문
gum	껌
glue	풀

■ Dialogue

너 몇 살이야?

난 일곱 살이야.

그는 몇 살이야?

그는 여섯 살이야.

■ Listen and repeat

① 너 몇 살이야?

② 다섯 살이에요.

③ 너 몇 살이야?

④ 난 아홉 살이야.

⑤ 너 몇 살이야?

⑥ 네 살.

■ Let's practice

A.

 2　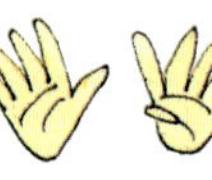 3　 1

B.

❶ seven

❷ three

❸ two

❹ ten

C.

4　　2　　1　　3

■ Let's sing

♪ 열 마리의 작은 강아지들

하나, 둘, 세 마리의 작은 강아지들.

넷, 다섯, 여섯 마리의 작은 강아지들.

일곱, 여덟, 아홉 마리의 작은 강아지들.

열 마리의 작은 강아지들.

UNIT1 Hello!

A.

❶ A: Goodbye.
  B: Bye, Olivia.
❷ A: Hello, Hannah.
  B: Hi, Ms. Smith.
❸ A: Hi, Joshua. How are you?
  B: I'm good. Thank you.

C.

❶ puppy ❷ pencil ❸ pan ❹ pig

UNIT2 Thank you!

A.

❶ A: Thank you.
  B: You're welcome.
❷ A: I'm sorry.
  B: That's all right.

C.

❶ ball ❷ bag ❸ bus ❹ bike

UNIT3 What is your name?

A.

❶ A: What's your name?
  B: I'm Hannah.
❷ A: What's your name?
  B: I'm Joshua.
❸ Hello, my name is Ethan.
❹ Hi, my name is Olivia.

C.

❶ tiger ❷ toy ❸ ten ❹ top

UNIT4 What is this?

A.

❶ A: What is that?
  B: That is a vase.
❷ A: What is this?
  B: This is a bag.
❸ A: What are these?
  B: These are pencils.

B.

❶ A: What is this?
  B: This is a cap.
❷ A: What is that?
  B: That is a television.
❸ A: What is that?
  B: That is a telephone.

C.

❶ duck ❷ doll ❸ desk ❹ dog

UNIT5 Is it a book?

A.

❶ Is it a book?
❷ Is it a car?
❸ Is it a dog?

C.

❶ fox   ❷ fish   ❸ fan   ❹ fork

UNIT6　Who is he?

A.

❶ A: Who is he?
B: He is my grandfather.
❷ A: Who is she?
B: She is my mom.
❸ A: Who are they?
B: They are my brothers.

C.

❶ van   ❷ vase   ❸ violin   ❹ vest

UNIT7　What color is it?

A.

❶ A: What color is it?
B: It's red.
❷ A: What color is it?
B: It's green.
❸ A: What color is it?
B: It's black.
❹ A: What color is it?
B: It's yellow.

C.

❶ sun   ❷ six   ❸ star   ❹ sit

UNIT8　What do you like?

A.

❶ A: What do you like?
B: I like ice cream.

❷ A: What do you like?
B: I like cookies.
❸ A: What do you like?
B: I like milk.

C.

❶ zipper   ❷ zebra   ❸ zoo   ❹ zero

UNIT9　Do you like oranges?

A.

❶ A: Do you like oranges?
B: Yes, I do.
❷ A: Do you like bananas?
B: Yes, I do.
❸ A: Do you like pears?
B: No, I don't. I like apples.

C.

❶ car   ❷ king   ❸ cat   ❹ key

UNIT10　How old are you?

A.

❶ A: How old are you?
B: I'm ten.
❷ A: How old are you?
B: I'm five years old.
❸ A: How old are you?
B: I'm nine.

C.

❶ glue   ❷ game   ❸ goat   ❹ girl

Index

Author **SunYoung Hyun**

Teaching English at private English Institute for 5 years
Certificate in TESOL
(Hanyang University and University of Oregon Joint TESOL Program)
BA both in French and Spanish Hankuk University of Foreign Studies
Certificate of English Language Institute in Queen's College in N.Y.

Supervisor **Keith Milling**

Teaching English at Hanyang University since 2001
MA in Linguistics with TESOL Concentration Northeastern Illinois University
BS in Speech and Hearing Science University of Illinois at Urbana-Champaign

Hey Kids! ❶

11th Printing	2019. 07. 25
Author	SunYoung Hyun
Supervisor	Keith Milling
Illustrator	EunJeong Kim
Publisher	KiSeon Lee
Publishing Company	JPLUS Publishing Co.
Address	31Street-62, Worldcup-Ro, Mapo-gu, Seoul, Korea
Telephone	02-332-8320
Fax	02-332-8321
Web Site	www.jplus114.com
Registration Number	10-1680
Registration Date	1998.12.09
ISBN	978-89-92215-07-7

UNIT3 P.31

UNIT9 P.81

UNIT4 P.39

    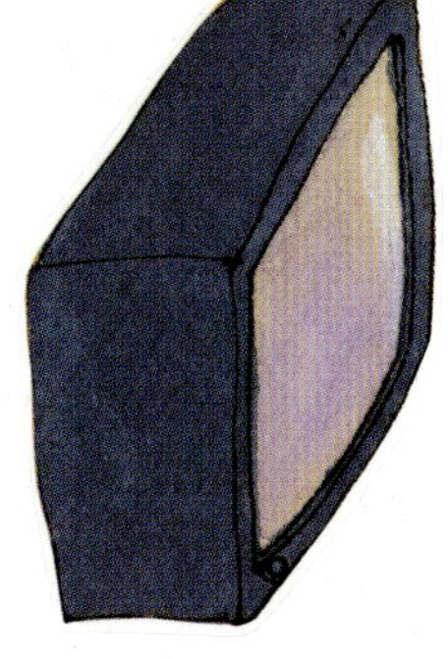

UNIT4 P.40

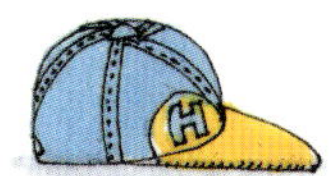   

UNIT6 P.55

UNIT7 P.64

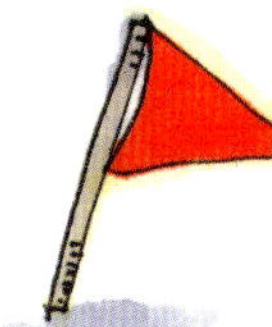 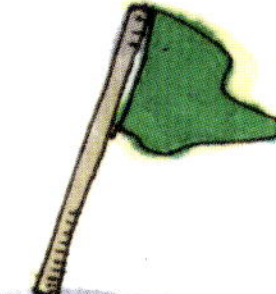  

UNIT9 P.79

  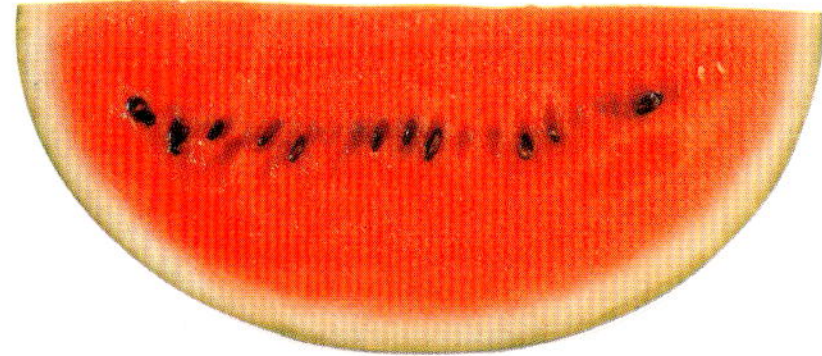

Joshua

Hannah

Olivia

Ethan

Ms. Smith

Dusty

You're welcome!

Thank you!

09

10

11

12

13

14

15

16

That's
all right!

I'm sorry!

cap

bag

notebook

pencil

vase

chair

book

television

taxi

bus

dog

cat

apple

desk

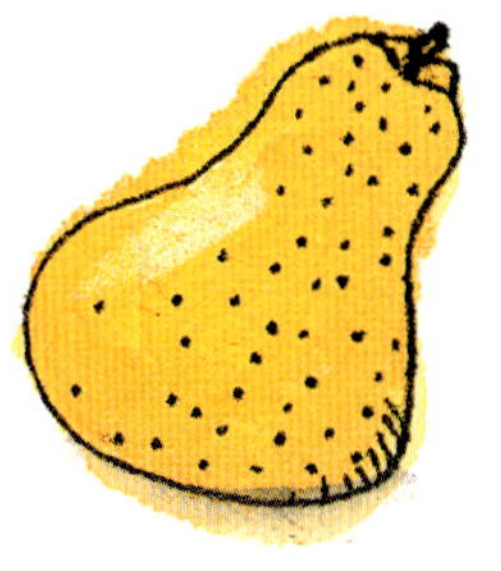

25

26

27

28

29

30

31

32

father

pear

grandfather

mother

sister

grandmother

cousin

brother

33

34

35

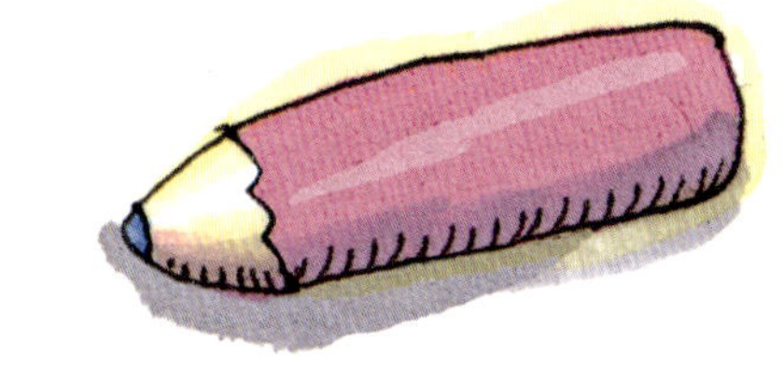

36

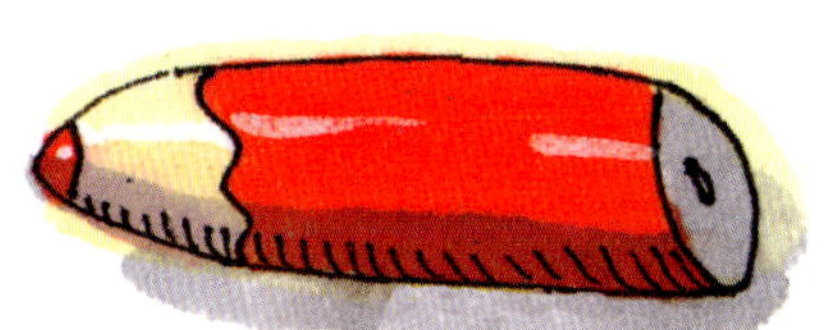

37

38

39

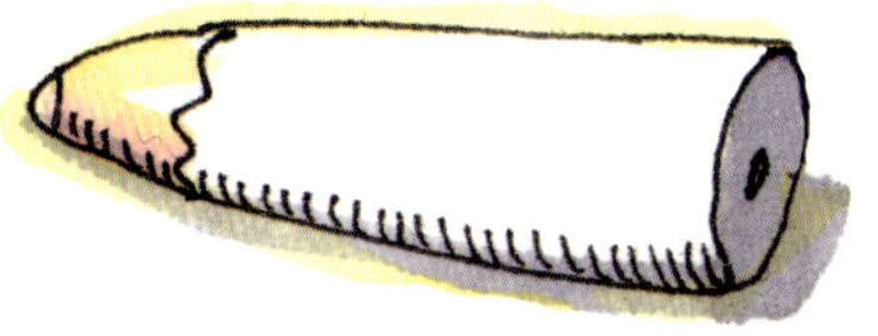

40

blue

baby sister

pink

green

yellow

red

white

black

41

42

43

44

45

46

47

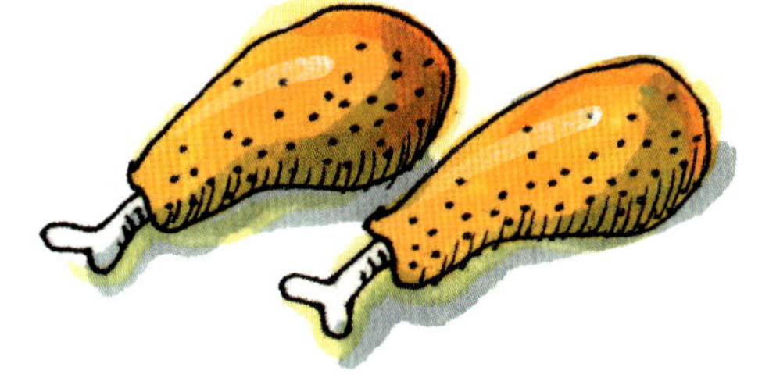

48

orange

purple

ice cream

brown

pizza

hamburger

milk

chicken

49

50

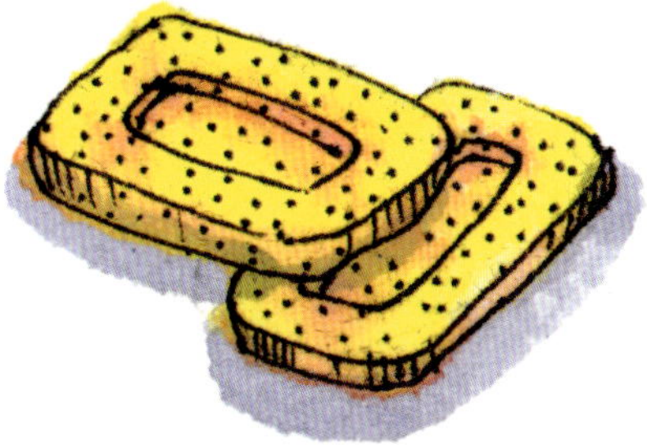

51

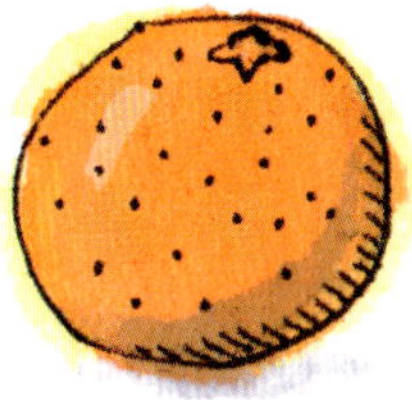

52

53

54

55

56

cookies

cake

banana

orange

peach

grape

kiwi

watermelon

strawberry

pineapple

two

one

four

three

six

five

7

8

9

10

eight

seven

ten

nine